Where Two or Three Are Gathered

Transforming the Parish through Communities of Practice

JANE E. REGAN

Paulist Press
New York / Mahwah, NJ

Cover image by FMonkey Crazy Jump / Shutterstock.com
Cover and book design by Sharyn Banks

Library of Congress Cataloging-in-Publication Data

Names: Regan, Jane E., author.
Title: Where two or three are gathered : transforming the parish through communities of practice / Jane E. Regan.
Description: New York : Paulist Press, 2016. | Includes bibliographical references.
Identifiers: LCCN 2016000388 (print) | LCCN 2016015304 (ebook) | ISBN 9780809149988 (pbk. : alk. paper) | ISBN 9781587686252 (Ebook)
Subjects: LCSH: Parishes. | Pastoral theology—Catholic Church. | Church management. | Church work—Catholic Church. | Communities—Religious aspects—Catholic Church.
Classification: LCC BX1913 .R388 2016 (print) | LCC BX1913 (ebook) | DDC 253/.32—dc23
LC record available at https://lccn.loc.gov/2016000388

ISBN 978-0-8091-4998-8 (paperback)
ISBN 978-1-58768-625-2 (e-book)

Published by Paulist Press
997 Macarthur Boulevard
Mahwah, New Jersey 07430

www.paulistpress.com

Printed and bound in the
United States of America

To my daughters
Catherine V. Regan
and
Natalya J. Regan
(1989–2013)

CONTENTS

ACKNOWLEDGMENTS

As is the case for many books, particularly those long in the writing as this one has been, this work has grown from a fairly simple idea written up as an essay for use in teaching, to a more extensive examination of themes and insights that evolved through conversation with a variety of people. Three different but complementary clusters influenced my writing of this book.

The first would be my students, to whom I introduced the core ideas of this book in a course that I have been teaching for several years: Adult Believers in a Postmodern Context. Many of the graduate students, whom I have the good fortune to teach at the School of Theology and Ministry at Boston College, bring rich and diverse experience to the conversation. The ideas related to "communities of practice"—both the theoretical and practical— set the foundations for the book. Their encouragement throughout the writing process was important, even though the ever present question, "Is the book out yet?" in the years after their class was more challenging.

The second cluster would be my friends and colleagues, who read chapters of the work at various stages and listened attentively and encouragingly as I talked through some element or idea. Particular acknowledgment goes to Mimi Bitzan, Thomas Groome, Theresa O'Keefe, and Barbara Radtke. Many thanks for your time and wisdom.

And the third is the large group of people with whom I have had the good fortune to minister as religious educator these past many years. While I may have been the one responsible for faith formation—whether as DRE at St. Patrick's in Fayetteville, North

Carolina, or at St. Patrick's in Chicopee, Massachusetts; or as part of the religious education staff for the diocese of Springfield, Massachusetts, or the archdiocese of Washington, DC; or as consultant or presenter in dioceses across the United States; or as presenter to the parents of children preparing for first sacraments in my home parish of St. Timothy's, Massachusetts—I was nonetheless formed in my own faith through those experiences. While I may not have yet been thinking in terms of "communities of practice," my identity and faith were fashioned by the gatherings of catechists or advisory boards or staff members with whom I met and worked and prayed. For all of these people and faith communities, I am grateful.

Part One

INTRODUCTION

Some years ago following my return from Russia with my older daughter, Natalya, whom I had adopted at the age of four, there were many "firsts" as she began to experience life and culture in the United States. One of these was her first visit to a large grocery store. As we entered the store, she immediately caught sight of the mesmerizing colors of the gumball machines. She dashed over to them and looked at me hopefully, though I'm sure she had no idea what they were. I walked over to her and bent down, put my arm on her shoulder, gently shook my head and said, "Regans don't buy gum from gumball machines." She looked back at them wistfully as we walked away to do our shopping. This was repeated a few times until eventually Natalya would enter the grocery store with me with barely a glance at the colorful collection.

A year-and-a-half later, her younger sister arrived at the age of two, also from Russia, to join our family. A few days after she arrived, we again headed to the grocery store for needed supplies. As we walked into the store, Natalya took Catie by the hand and walked her over to the line of gumball machines. She stooped down next to her, put her hand on her shoulder, and said a bit sadly, "Regans don't buy gum from gumball machines." With that comment, Natalya passed on to Catie something of what she had learned about what it means to live as a Regan.

Put simply, this book is about how we learn what it means to live as Christians and how we pass that meaning or tradition on to others. In this case, the focus is not on how we do these things as children, but how we learn and pass it on as adults; that is, how do we learn to live as adult Christians in our contemporary context?

Natalya and Catie learned what it meant to live as Regans by hanging out with Regans, by learning our habits and patterns, by engaging with the world the way Regans do. Sometimes that involved direct instruction—"Regans don't buy gum from gumball machines"—but more often, it was acquired in the rhythm of life.

The same is true for Christians. We learn what it means to be a Christian by hanging out with other Christians, by living out the Christian patterns and practices, by engaging with the world the way Christians do. Sometimes this involves direct instruction, but more often, it is simply nurtured and developed in the rhythm of life.

One of the settings in which Christians spend time with other Christians is in the context of the local parish. This is certainly a primary context where people have explicit connection with other believers. However, beyond the Sunday liturgy, adults also collaborate on various committees and councils and advisory boards, such as the finance committee, the social justice committee, and the adult education advisory board, and they come together as catechists or lectors or in the youth ministry program. It is this second setting that I am interested in examining in this book—how the experience of being about the work of the parish, both within and outside its boundaries, can be a context through which people's faith is enhanced and strengthened.

In doing this, I draw upon resources not only from the theological disciplines but from education, the social sciences, and business. Whenever one writes a book at the intersection of practice and theory, and drawing on a diversity of sources, there are some fundamental presumptions that stand behind the writing that may not always get full articulation. Here are four of the key presumptions upon which this book rests:

The church is more than a sociological reality. Throughout the text, I draw upon business and education models or approaches. While I'm convinced that these can serve as helpful tools for analyzing dynamics that are at play within parish communities, they don't say everything about a parish or the nature of the church. Central to any discussion of invigorating parish life or strengthening the faith of its members rests on the conviction of the work of the Holy Spirit in the process of renewal and conversion.

An ecclesiology is presumed but not explicitly named. Building on the ecclesiology reflected in the documents of the Second Vatican Council, this book places an emphasis on the radical challenge and grace of baptism, the universal call to holiness, the centrality of a sacramental view of the world, and the fundamental responsibility of all members of the church to be about the work of evangelization.

Each parish has a distinctive nature. Throughout the text, examples and approaches reflect the theoretical framework along with my experience in pastoral ministry and as a parishioner. Additionally, there are valuable insights gained from my work as a professor of religious education and practical theology where I have had the opportunity to teach and learn from people who have worked in a wide range of pastoral settings both nationally and around the world. That being said, the usefulness of a particular idea in a specific locale can only be established by those living and working in that context. In many ways, the examples and approaches are designed to trigger your own imagining for your parish and to encourage you to try out new ideas in your context and setting.

People can and will accept (if not embrace) change. With a new perspective, we consider different ways that the multiple committees, advisory boards, and groups of people can accomplish their work and shape the life of the parish. Thinking of them beyond their functional role and seeing their potential as a context and catalyst for enhancing the faith life and evangelizing capacity of their members may well require changes in the way these groups are viewed and organized. Long-standing modes of operating and styles of organization may need to be reconsidered. Change experts tell us that changes are made easier when (1) people are made aware of the changes and the rationale for them; (2) they are engaged in the conversation of how and why the changes are taking place; and (3) they sense that the challenge in making changes is recognized and that those in authority support them. Inviting people to think differently about the roles they play in the parish and the expectations that those roles might encompass takes time, tact, and tenacity. But it can happen!

Reflective of these presumptions, the book unfolds in two parts. Part one consists of three chapters. Chapter one invites us to reflect on the components of Christian faith and the ways they can be nurtured within the life of the parish. First, we examine the following fundamental elements: our relationship with Jesus, our affiliation with the Christian community, and our commitment to the wider mission of the church. Second, we focus on the call to evangelization that flows from Christian faith, analyzing the term *evangelization* and what it means in contemporary church documents and how it relates to the "new evangelization." To be an evangelizing agent is the primary responsibility of the Christian community; how we enhance people's capacity for evangelization is the focus of the book.

Chapter two examines the central notion of "communities of practice." Building on practice and research in business and education, the concept of communities of practice provides an alternative approach to the various committees and communities through which adults gather to accomplish the various work of the parish—the parish council, the catechists, the choir, the liturgy committee, the social justice committee, and so on. In this chapter, we also examine both the constitutive elements of these groups and the kind of learning and identity formation that takes place within them.

While one might easily argue that these communities of practice have a formative effect, the question addressed in chapter 3 is how are they *faith* formative? To answer this question, we need to explore the intentionality in how the groups are organized and facilitated. Furthermore, we need to examine their faith formative capacity: their role in welcoming new and renewing members, the connections that can be fostered among communities of practice, and the ways in which the gifts and talents of each of the members of these communities are recognized and enhanced. Part two develops these ideas further by considering the central place of hospitality, conversation, followership, and discernment within these communities.

To foster a mature, evangelizing community of adult believers requires the commitment and active engagement of all members of the pastoral staff, and indeed of the whole parish. This book presents how such efforts might be marshaled and the vision given expression. Like all actions of a faith community, we rely on faith in God's ever present offer of grace, hope in the working of the Spirit in the lives of this particular community of believers, and love for the faith-filled but very human gathering of folks who are about the important work of living in such a way as to serve as signs of God's loving action in the world. May you continue to become such a community!

Chapter 1

AN EVANGELIZING FAITH

How do we come to "have faith," that is, how do we make sense of our world and find meaning in our lives with reference to a center of value and power outside of ourselves? As Christians, how do we come to make sense of our world and find meaning in reference to the God expressed to us through Jesus? Here are three stories that may help answer these questions. The first is from a first-year college student, Ryan, reflecting on an experience that had a positive effect on his faith.[1]

> One event that had a positive impact on my faith was my Confirmation retreat when I was in tenth grade. I really did not want to go—it was scheduled from Saturday afternoon through to the regular Sunday evening Mass at 5:00 p.m. in the parish and that seemed like a very long time to me. The most important part of the retreat for me was Saturday night when we had to go to confession. I hadn't been to confession since I was little—maybe third or fourth grade, so I was a bit apprehensive. I didn't know what to expect. I'm not sure if this is always how it happens, but for the retreat they had a series of readings—stories about Jesus forgiving people. I remember that one about the Prodigal Son and another about Zacchaeus. After each story, someone got up—one of the group leaders or an older high school kid—and related the story to their lives. Each one talked about a time when they had been forgiven, a time when they really messed up or broke somebody's trust. They talked about how they had been forgiven by their parents

or a friend. But they also talked about how they had experienced the forgiveness of Jesus. I had never actually heard anyone talk about that before. I know we have to ask God for forgiveness, but they made it sound so personal. Like Jesus really cared about them. That thought stayed with me all that night and into the next day. I remember talking with one of the group leaders on Sunday afternoon—one of the ones who had spoken on Saturday night. That was really helpful. At Mass that evening back at the parish, things just seemed different—I felt different: more aware of Jesus being present; more conscious of someone actually hearing the prayers I said. It felt like Jesus really cared about me, too.

For Ryan, having faith means having a personal relationship with Jesus. It is by encountering Jesus through other people and in the sacraments that Ryan's faith is renewed. He begins to see his life and understand the things that happen in the context of the care that he believes Jesus has for him.

Melissa presents another angle on the question of faith. A single mom of a seven-year-old daughter, Melissa credits the parish program for families with children preparing for first communion with reconnecting her with her faith and with the parish community. Her story is similar to many others'.

David and I divorced when Cara was three—in some ways, it is amazing that we lasted that long, but that's a story for another time. I had been going to Mass fairly regularly before that, but after the divorce, I felt really uncomfortable about going. Over time, Sunday morning became like Saturday morning—an opportunity to spend time with Cara and to do errands. But, sooner than I thought possible, Cara was going into second grade and I had to start thinking about her First Communion. It's funny: even though we weren't going to Mass, it seemed really important to me to have Cara receive her First Communion. I kind of knew there were some meetings for parents, so I wasn't totally surprised when I got the schedule of meetings—four spread out over the year.

The first meeting was really quite different from what I thought it would be: I thought we'd be talking about what the children were learning or about what we had to do to get them ready. Instead, it was really about my faith and ways that I could help it grow. I was afraid that I wouldn't know things that I should know about church teaching and things, but that wasn't really what the session was about.

While the speakers were good, the part I enjoyed the most was the small group discussions. It was good to hear the questions and concerns that other parents had; I wasn't even the only one who was divorced. I realized after the second session that this was the first time I'd had the opportunity to talk about my faith since I was in high school!

Slowly I began to participate more in things at the parish: all the second grade families were invited to an Advent event where we made Advent wreaths and learned some things about the seasons. During Lent, I actually went to an adult class by myself—I never would have done that if I hadn't met people through the Eucharist program.

If I were to say the one thing I learned during the past year with Cara is that being part of a community is really important to my faith. Making the commitment to go to Mass every Sunday (when we can) has made a big difference in how I think about myself, my connection to the parish, and my relationship with God.

For Melissa, faith is given expression and strengthened through the life of the community. Through the program, she experiences a sense of being welcomed in the parish. The opportunity to talk with other adults about their children, about what's important to them, and about their faith gave Melissa a chance to reflect on her own faith in a way that she had never done as an adult. Her membership and commitment to a faith community serve as a foundation for her growing faith. It has been through her affiliation with the community that she has begun to look at the world and her life through a new lens, one that is more rooted in God.

Tom and Joanne tell a different story. Now in their mid-seventies, they speak of faith in terms of service. They have been members of the same parish since they were first married and moved into the area. They raised their children in the parish—three boys now all grown and moved away. They were involved in the parish: they went to church every Sunday; Joanne taught in the religious education program as the boys went through the various grades; Tom helped out at the annual Fall Bazaar and served on the parish council for a couple of terms. Joanne tells their story:

> Once the boys were confirmed and had graduated and went on to college, it seemed that there really wasn't anything to do in the parish if you didn't have kids around. Of course, there were Bible study groups and a prayer group; I know there were some other committees and things, but nothing that Tom and I thought would be interesting. And so our connection with our faith kind of slacked off; our participation in the parish became fairly minimal.
>
> The change, I would say, happened when Tom retired. A man from church whom we had known in the past fairly well through parish activities called and asked Tom if he would be interested in bringing meals a couple of afternoons a week to people who were homebound. The call came at a perfect time as Tom was looking for something to do with his free time. As he became involved in this work—ministry really—he also had the opportunity to meet one morning a week with the six or seven other people from the parish who were delivering meals. While part of the meeting addressed logistics and who would bring

dinner to whom, the beginning of each meeting was spent in prayer and in talking about articles or short readings that they received each week.

Tom loved delivering meals and looked forward to the weekly meeting with the group. He would bring home the articles and we'd talk about them together. When I retired last year, getting involved in this ministry was one of my priorities. I love meeting the people to whom we deliver the meals, chatting with them about their lives and grown children. Through the weekly meetings with the rest of the group, both Tom and I feel more connected to the life of the parish again. It has helped us see the connection between going to Mass on Sunday and caring for and serving others.

For Joanne, her faith was expressed and enhanced in service with and for others. It was the people she got to know both in the parish and in the community that called her to service and thus enlivened her faith.

For each of these Catholics, the experience of faith, of growing in faith, is rooted in various aspects of our common faith journey: our relationship with Jesus, our affiliation with and commitment to the faith community, and our participation in the church's mission of service and justice. At different times in our lives and in light of distinct experiences, we may emphasize one dimension over the other. But it is in the essential interconnection of these three elements that the depth of Christian faith is found and the substance of our individual and communal faith stories can be told.

Let us now examine the dynamic relationship among these three elements, first by highlighting their presence in the early Christian community. We then focus on the contemporary setting by tracing the presence of these same components—*relationship with Jesus, commitment to a faith community, and participation in the church's mission*—in our understanding of evangelization as it is expressed by the Second Vatican Council.

"COME, FOLLOW ME"

These were the words Peter and his brother Andrew heard as they were casting nets into the sea; their response: "Immediately they left their nets and followed him" (Matt 4:20). The brothers James and John heard the same call as they were tending their boats: "Immediately they left the boat and their father, and followed him" (Matt 4:22). Not by the sea but in a tax collector's booth, Matthew heard Jesus' invitation, "and he got up, left everything, and followed him" (Luke 5:28).

These stories, passed down within the Christian community and articulated in some form in each of the Gospels, highlight the fundamentally personal nature of this invitation. Whatever prior interaction these early followers had with Jesus, what is clear is that there is a point of invitation and of decision and commitment: Jesus invited them to follow him, they left their work and lives, and they followed him.

These invitations didn't always result in leaving things behind to respond to the call. Take, for example, the story of the rich young man that is told in Mark 10. The story begins at the initiation of the rich young man; perhaps he was a "seeker," attempting to find meaning in a world fraught with challenges. Or perhaps he was trying to justify his lifestyle or check to be sure that he had done what is needed to get to heaven (v. 17). Jesus' response (v. 19) seems a little terse: "You know the commandments." And then he went on to name the basics. The rich man agreed and said that he had been following these all his life. The evangelist Mark then wrote,

> Jesus, looking at him, loved him and said, "You lack one thing; go, sell what you own, and give the money to the poor, and you will have treasure in heaven; then come, follow me." When he heard this, he was shocked and went away grieving, for he had many possessions. (vv. 21–22)

While the call to "Come, follow me" was offered to the rich man, his response at that point was not to leave everything and follow Jesus; rather, he went away sad. For him, the invitation to enter into a personal relationship with Jesus was simply too costly.

For the early disciples, however, responding to the invitation to follow Jesus involved entering into a relationship with Jesus rooted in each one's personal encounter with him. This relationship is the taproot from which evolved their identity, their relationship with one another, and their stance toward the world.

"LOVE ONE ANOTHER"

In the account of the Last Supper in John's Gospel, Jesus explicitly shifts the focus from each disciple's relationship with him to their relationship to one another in him:

> I ask not only on behalf of these, but also on behalf of those who will believe in me through their word, that they may all be one. As you, Father, are in me and I am in you, may they also be in us, so that the world may believe that you have sent me. The glory that you have given me I have given them, so that they may be one, as we are one, I in them and you in me, that they may become completely one, so that the world may know that you have sent me and have loved them even as you have loved me. (John 17:20–23)

Throughout this "high priestly prayer" is the injunction to love one another in response to God's love. The fundamental role of the disciples shifts from following Jesus to taking responsibility to care for one another and thereby witnessing to the saving action of God in Jesus.

Sustained by their experiences with Jesus and their memory of his words and works, the disciples turned their focus to those who found in Jesus and his message the same reason for hope that the disciples had found. In the Acts of the Apostles, written about the same time as the Gospel of Luke, around 80–90 CE, an image of the early community in Jerusalem emerges: "They devoted themselves to the apostles' teaching and fellowship, to the breaking of bread and the prayers" (Acts 2:42).

As described in Acts,[2] three characteristics shaped the nascent life of the Christian community: a fundamental reliance on the teaching of the apostles; affiliation with the Temple continued while the "breaking of bread" took place in their homes; and all things were held in common with a distribution of the wealth of the community such that the needs of the poor were addressed. These three dimensions of community life can be found throughout the writings of the early church.

At times, these three aspects of community life are highlighted because of their absence. For example, in 1 Corinthians 11 and 12, Paul gives the church in Corinth explicit instructions on how the members should treat one another, particularly in light of the celebration of the Eucharist. From Paul's perspective, how they treat one another—the life of the community—is an essential component to living as Jesus called them to live.

"GLAD TIDINGS TO THE POOR"

In addition to the relationship with Jesus and an affiliation with those gathered in his name, emphasis was also placed on the necessity of looking beyond the community to the wider world that still awaited the proclamation of the good news. The "Great Commission" is found in the closing verses of Matthew's Gospel:

> Go therefore and make disciples of all nations, baptizing them in the name of the Father and of the Son and of the Holy Spirit, and teaching them to obey everything that I have commanded you. And remember, I am with you always, to the end of the age. (Matt 28:19–20)

Making disciples is a two-step process: baptizing them and teaching them. In addition to bringing them into the unity of the Trinity embodied in the life of the Christian community, Jesus' followers are also charged with teaching the new disciples the way of life that was taught by Jesus in words and actions.

One of the earliest expressions of the way of life ushered in by Jesus' coming is found in one of the opening pericopes in the Gospel of Luke concerning Jesus' ministry. Here, Jesus has returned from forty days in the desert and goes to Nazareth where, he "went to the synagogue on the sabbath day, as was his custom" (Luke 4:16). When handed the scroll of the Prophet Isaiah to read, Jesus unrolled it and read,

> "The Spirit of the Lord is upon me,
>> because he has anointed me to bring good news to
>>> the poor.
> He has sent me to proclaim release to the captives
>> and recovery of sight to the blind, to let the
>>> oppressed go free,
> to proclaim the year of the Lord's favor."
>
> (Luke 4:18–19)

After returning the scroll, Jesus sat down and said, "Today this scripture has been fulfilled in your hearing" (v. 21).

Throughout Luke's Gospel, and echoed in the other three, the fundamental vision that Jesus lived throughout his own life and taught his disciples through word and action is to bring justice and freedom to those who are oppressed in all of the ways in which people experience oppression. This is what the disciples learned from Jesus; this is what they were to teach those who were to be baptized in Jesus' name. It is not sufficient to gather as a community in the warmth of human affection: the early Christian community always gathered in order to be sent to teach and live out the saving action of God proclaimed and effected in Jesus.

These three themes—relationship with Jesus, affiliation with and commitment to the Christian community, and participation in the mission of the church—point to the way we experience *and* express our faith, that is, how we grow in our capacity to make meaning of our lives in the context of that which transcends us.[3] Through our relationships with Jesus Christ and the Christian community, as well as our involvement in the proclamation of the reign of God, we are formed as believers. We see and engage with the world through the lens of the life, death, and resurrection of Jesus. Jesus' life revealed to us the reality of God as creator and loving parent; Jesus' presence continues to be manifest to us today through the ongoing work of the Holy Spirit. In this sense, we come to know ourselves as believers through our participation in the Trinity—Creator, Redeemer, and Sanctifier.

These three interrelated dimensions are the foundations of an adult faith that is vibrant and fruitful; a faith that is lived out in effective discipleship. A discipleship rooted in relationship with Jesus and committed to the Christian community has an outward orientation. Just as Jesus gathered the apostles around him in order to prepare them to be sent forth to proclaim the gospel, disciples today are gathered to be sent out as agents of evangelization. To speak of adult faith is to speak of evangelizing faith.

Conversation and Reflection

1. Share an experience that has strengthened your faith as an adult.

2. In what ways are the three key elements—relationship with Jesus, affiliation with a Christian community, and participation in the mission of the church—part of your own faith development?

3. What opportunities are available to adults in your pastoral setting to enhance their relationship with Jesus, to live out their commitment to the parish, and to engage in action in service of the church's mission in the world?

EVANGELIZATION

Since the promulgation of the documents of Vatican II, there has been a growing consciousness of the nature, role, and expression of evangelization in the life of the church and its members. With increasing clarity, ecclesial documents have articulated the place of evangelization at the heart of the church's mission. Let us examine these documents to get an understanding of evangelization as it has unfolded and a sense of the new evangelization.

As with most pastoral and theological issues within the Roman Catholic Church today, we begin with reference to Vatican Council II. The general mindset in many of the Council's documents was the foundation for a renewal of the church's mission to evangelize and of the nature of evangelization itself. This is particularly true of the documents that address the nature and role of the church itself: *Lumen Gentium* and *Gaudium et Spes*. However, the foundational text for our understanding of evangelization is *Ad Gentes*.[4] While our understanding of evangelization has broadened since the writing of *Ad Gentes*, this document effectively reflects the understanding of evangelization operative at the time of the Council. Two themes, in particular, are present in the document and are echoed in later statements.

The first theme is the recognition that evangelization is a complex reality, rooted in the culture and responsive to the needs of the setting. The document makes clear the three dimensions of evangelization: witnessing through actions of charity and justice, proclaiming, and establishing vibrant communities of faith. The second significant theme is its affirmation that evangelization is the responsibility of all the members of the church: "The work of evangelization is a basic duty of the People of God" (no. 35), and, therefore, the formation of the laity is of paramount importance (no. 21).

Ten years after the promulgation of *Ad Gentes*, Pope Paul VI wrote the "Apostolic Exhortation on Evangelization," *Evangelii Nuntiandi* (EN),[5] in light of the 1974 synod on evangelization. At the heart of the document is this statement:

We wish to confirm once more that the task of evangelizing all people constitutes the essential mission of the
Church. It is a task and mission which the vast and pro-
found changes of present-day society make all the more
urgent. Evangelizing is in fact the grace and vocation
proper to the Church, her deepest identity. She exists in
order to evangelize....(no. 14)

The reason for the church's being is to be an agent of evangelization. Pope Paul VI goes on to define evangelization as "bringing the Good News into all the strata of humanity, and through its
influence transforming humanity from within and making it new"
(no. 18). He also makes the point that the church is both evangelizer and always in need of evangelization (no. 15). The ongoing
renewal of the church is essential to its ability to fulfill God's fundamental mission for it—to proclaim the gospel.

Another synod that contributed to our understanding of
evangelization was held in 1977; its theme was catechesis with a
particular focus on the catechesis of children and youth. In 1979,
Pope John Paul II issued *Catechesi Tradendae* (CT), the "Apostolic
Exhortation on Catechesis."[6] Similar to the concepts presented in
EN, CT also affirms the centrality of evangelization to the life of
the church. In CT, the multifaceted nature of evangelization is
highlighted; Pope John Paul II speaks of various moments of evangelization: "Evangelization...is a rich, complex and dynamic reality, made up of elements, or one could say moments, that are
essential and different from each other, and that must all be kept
in view simultaneously" (no. 18). He then goes on to say,
"Catechesis is one of these moments—a very remarkable one—in
the whole process of evangelization." Here, evangelization is seen
as the foundation for the pastoral life of the church; all activities—
preaching, liturgy, action for justice, community—make sense in
light of the call to evangelize.

The next document, *Christifideles Laici* (CL), the "Apostolic
Exhortation on the Laity,"[7] comes ten years after CT. Published in
1988, it is the result of a synod of bishops that met to discuss the

role of the laity, and is one of the first documents to introduce the concept of re-evangelization, later to be called new evangelization. Reflecting on the reality of de-Christianized contexts and the rise of secularism, Pope John Paul II calls for a re-evangelization, which begins with addressing the Christian community itself. We must "first remake the Christian fabric of the ecclesial community itself" so that it can reflect what it means to live in Christ (no. 34).

In 1991, Pope John Paul II promulgated the encyclical *Redemptoris Missio* (RM), "On the Church's Mission Activity."[8] This document included a clear articulation of the meaning of "new evangelization" and the challenge that it holds for the church. While not wanting to lose focus on the responsibility of the church to proclaim the gospel to those who have never heard it, this document also makes the case for the importance of a new evangelization addressed to the baptized of all ages who have become distant from the church and Christ's teachings. One of the clarifying contributions of this document is the discussion of the three situations in which evangelization is needed. The first concerns "peoples, groups, and socio-cultural contexts in which Christ and his gospel are not known, or which lack Christian communities sufficiently mature to be able to incarnate the faith in their own environment and proclaim it to other groups" (no. 33). This is the classic understanding of evangelization *ad gentes* (i.e., to the nations). The second situation focuses on the vibrant Christian communities that are able to support the faith life of their members and provide a context where children can grow up in the faith. Here evangelization takes place in the regular pastoral life of the church. The third situation is "where entire groups of the baptized have lost a living sense of the faith, or even no longer consider themselves members of the Church, and live a life far removed from Christ and his Gospel. In this case what is needed is a 'new evangelization' or a 're-evangelization'"(no. 33). We return to this topic below.

A further document that addresses the place of evangelization in the life of the church is the General Directory for Catechesis (GDC),[9] published in 1998 by the Congregation for the Clergy, which has responsibility for overseeing catechesis.[10] In many ways, the GDC provides a summative statement outlining the church's understanding of evangelization, weaving together many of the insights from the other documents we have examined. It is particularly compelling in its discussion of the multifaceted nature of evangelization and the various ways in which it comes to expression. It describes evangelization as "a dynamic reality which contains within it interdependent activities which are to be kept in creative tension: witness and proclamation, word and sacrament, interior change and social transformation" (no. 46). The GDC details the various expressions of evangelization and the central role of catechesis, particularly adult catechesis.

This series of six documents outlines the evolution of evangelization over the past forty years. Let us now consider four general themes that develop across the texts of these documents.

Evangelization Is Connected to the Very Life and Identity of the Church

The very essence of the church is the sharing of the gospel with the world around us. As EN states and other documents echo, the church exists in order to evangelize. A Christian community cannot opt out of the work of proclaiming the gospel in word and action. To be a Christian community is to engage in evangelization.

Evangelization Is Multifaceted and Complex

Evangelization cannot be reduced to a set of tasks nor be assigned to a particular group within the parish. It has less to do with *what* the parish does and more with *how* the parish accomplishes its work. We can speak of the evangelizing catechists or the evangelizing liturgy group, evangelizing youth group or the evangelizing finance committee, and ultimately the evangelizing parish. In each case, those responsible for these aspects of church life engage in their endeavors with an eye toward how their actions, attitudes, and decisions contribute to bringing the message of the reign of God into the world around us.

Evangelization Is the Responsibility of the Church and All Its Members

In the past, one thought of the church's evangelizing activity as something done by missionaries in faraway places. The contemporary understanding rekindles our responsibility for sharing the message of Christ to all believers, regardless of place or position. Particular emphasis is placed on the role of laypersons who, through their jobs and families, have the prime opportunity to witness to the reality of the reign of God by how they live their lives and engage with others around them.

Evangelization Is Rooted in the Situation of Those Being Evangelized

Evangelization takes place in a particular time and place and is responsive to the experience of those being evangelized. This attention to setting is particularly important in engaging in the new evangelization. How we address those who were baptized but never catechized is going to be different from those who were raised in the church and actively decided to leave. The evangelizing work done with young adults is different from that done with adults whose children have grown and moved away, and it is different again from what has to happen with single mid-life adults who feel that faith communities have nothing to offer them. Consequently, it is clear that evangelization begins with listening to the stories and experiences of those being evangelized and proceeds from there.

THE CALL FOR A "NEW EVANGELIZATION"

The first use of the term "new evangelization" by Pope John Paul II can be traced back to 1983 in an address to the Latin

American bishops in which he called for a commitment to a new evangelization.[11] The situation in Latin America, according to John Paul II, called for a new approach to evangelization: "new in ardor, methods and expression." Subsequent to that meeting, he spoke in various settings around the world of the need for a new evangelization. Because the church faces myriad challenges—secularization, religious indifference, the growing chasm between rich and poor—there is a need for a renewal in evangelization.

With the 1991 encyclical, *Redemptoris Missio*, Pope John Paul II brought the concept of "new evangelization" into the broader ecclesial conversation. In that document, new evangelization was particularly directed at those baptized who hold faith at a purely cultural level and who do not integrate faith with life (RM 34). With this new evangelization, there is the invitation to those who, for a variety of reasons, have become distant from the faith and see belief and faith practices as exterior to themselves (GDC 58). This mode of evangelization is one of the three situations within which evangelization takes place: to those who have never heard the gospel, to those who are engaged in an active Christian community, and to those baptized who are not living lives marked by faith.

Both John Paul II and Benedict XVI recognized the complex nature of the new evangelization. While the proclamation of the gospel of Jesus Christ is essential, it must be matched by the witness of Christian living and the work to transform the social order. This necessarily calls for the renewal of faith among church members and a strengthening of their commitment to the work of evangelization; it is clear that evangelization must include the renewal of parish life.

In 2013, Pope Francis issued the Apostolic Exhortation *Evangelii Gaudium* (The Joy of the Gospel). Written following the 2012 synod on the new evangelization, the document begins with a challenge to all believers:

> The joy of the gospel fills the hearts and lives of all who encounter Jesus. Those who accept his offer of salvation are set free from sin, sorrow, inner emptiness and

loneliness. With Christ joy is constantly born anew. In this Exhortation I wish to encourage the Christian faithful to embark upon a new chapter of evangelization marked by this joy, while pointing out new paths for the Church's journey in years to come. (EG 1)

This challenge to participate in the work of evangelization begins with the invitation to enter into a "renewed personal encounter with Jesus Christ" (EG 3). This is seen as the source and inspiration for all forms of evangelization. At the same time, from the first pages of the text, it is clear that at the heart of the call to engage in evangelization is the need to renew the life of the church. "To make this missionary impulse ever more focused, generous and fruitful, I encourage each particular Church to undertake a resolute process of discernment, purification, and reform" (EG 30). Participating and building up the Christian community is an essential component of evangelization. But we build up the Christian community in service to the missionary task of the church. The themes that Francis chose to develop in some detail in this exhortation give an indication of the breadth of his understanding of how this "new chapter in evangelization" comes to expression: "the reform of the Church in her missionary outreach; the temptations faced by pastoral workers; the Church, understood as the entire People of God which evangelizes; the homily and its preparation; the inclusion of the poor in society; peace and dialogue within society; the spiritual motivations for mission" (EG 17). This evangelizing faith, rooted in our relationship with Jesus, nurtured within the Christian community, is ultimately in service to the world.

Conversation and Reflection

1. What new or renewed understanding of the nature and expression of evangelization has developed from your reading of this section?

2. What difference does it make to your ministry when understood as a constitutive element of evangelization?

3. The "new evangelization" includes both strengthening the living faith of the parish and reaching out to others. How do you see these two components coming to expression in your pastoral setting?

4. In what ways is your parish an evangelizing parish? In what ways might its evangelizing force be strengthened?

Christian faith has its foundation in a personal, intimate relationship with Jesus that is fostered through prayer (both personal and communal), scripture, and worship. While deeply personal, this relationship with Jesus is not individual alone; it is strengthened and celebrated through our affiliation with and commitment to the Christian community. Furthermore, it is through our membership within the Christian community that we are called to deepen and express our faith through engagement in the mission of the church. These three elements serve as the foundation of an adult faith, which, as we have seen, is also an evangelizing faith. How to enhance that faith for the work of evangelization is the focus of the rest of this book.

Chapter 2

COMMUNITIES OF PRACTICE

As we have just noted, the heart of the Christian life is relationship with Jesus, affiliation with the Christian community, and participation in the mission of the church; through them, we experience and express what it means to be a Christian. As we mature in these three elements, we come to see the world more clearly and respond to it through the lens of a Christian believer. Our relationship with Jesus, our affiliation with the Christian community, and our participation in the mission of the church become the source of meaning in our lives; through them, our lives become ever more meaningful. Furthermore, since they are at the heart of Christian faith, it follows that they need to be central to the process of forming our faith and to the work of catechesis that is lifelong and parish wide.

Consideration of the church documents on catechesis makes clear that the fundamental aim of catechesis is to place the believer in close relationship with Jesus. The *General Directory for Catechesis* (GDC)[1] states, "The definitive aim of catechesis is to put people not only in touch, but also in communion and intimacy, with Jesus Christ" (no. 80). These documents also stress that catechesis happens in and through the life of the community. As we participate in the community's believing, celebrating, living, and proclaiming the Christian message, our own faith is strengthened and enhanced, and we, in turn, enhance the faith of others. And while the goal of catechesis is not to make smarter, nicer Christians—though that would be lovely—the goal of catechesis is to shape an evangelizing church with members who are able to give witness to the gospel through their lives, and are always

27

"ready to make [their] defense to anyone who demands from [them] an accounting for the hope that is in [them]" (1 Pet 3:15).

It is important to call to mind the centrality of evangelization to the life and vitality of the church. One of the primary documents on evangelization, the "Apostolic Exhortation on Evangelization" (*Evangelii Nuntiandi*), makes clear that the church's reason for being is rooted in evangelization: "Evangelizing is, in fact, the grace and vocation proper to the Church, her deepest identity. She exists in order to evangelize" (no. 14). Everything that is done within the life of the church is shaped by this call to evangelize—to give witness in word and action to the saving grace of God expressed in Jesus. Catechesis is to prepare us for this work.

While this understanding of evangelization is all well and good, how does it happen? How do we develop in our adults, youth, and children an awareness of the presence of Jesus in their lives so that this relationship becomes central to them? How do we enrich people's engagement with the life of the parish so that Sunday liturgy is the peak of their participation in the faith community rather than the sum total of it? And how do we direct the energy and imagination in the faith community from being directed inward to outward?

These are challenging questions that evade easy answers and can never be fully addressed by a new program or lecture series. But they are at the heart of the work, not only of religious education, but of the whole life of the parish. Consequently, it is essential that we look beyond what is generally termed *religious education* and look instead to the life of the parish for the means to respond to these challenges.

Indeed, it is our relationship with Jesus, our commitment to the community of faith, and our capacity to participate in the mission of the church—that is, our life of faith—that is fostered and enhanced by our connectivity with smaller groupings within the parish community. Many people involved with various kinds of small, faith-sharing groups would affirm this principle, and certainly those groups continue to be sources of faith and life within many parish communities. However, let's consider these smaller groups from a somewhat different angle. Here, we are not so much suggesting that we form faith sharing groups, but rather consider the groups that are already present in our parishes as possible contexts for fostering and enhancing mature faith.

Let's consider the parish "St. Odo the Good," for example. Like many parishes, St. Odo the Good has a pastoral staff, catechists, a liturgical group, a parish council, finance council, and a Bible study group. There is also a team responsible for the Rite of Christian Initiation of Adults (RCIA), a youth ministry advisory team, a social justice committee, and a welcome committee that organizes coffee and doughnuts after Mass on Sunday. If you were to list all the groups that gather under the general rubric of St. Odo the Good parish, you might be amazed. When these groups meet, they each do many of the same things: to a greater or lesser degree, they all talk, discuss, debate, argue, and gossip; they keep track of decisions and change their minds; accomplish set tasks; talk about the parish; reminisce and have coffee. Each time one of these groups meets, it has a particular task to accomplish. For example, the catechists might meet to plan the next set of sessions for their grade level or discuss a multigenerational gathering planned for Advent; the parish council might meet to discuss ways of collaborating with neighboring parishes in addressing the pastoral needs of youth or make plans for how best to welcome new members of the parish; the eucharistic ministers might gather to discuss the way scheduling is done or talk about a new process for the distribution of communion, and the list goes on.

Similarly, while each group has a particular task to accomplish at a specific meeting, there is also an overarching "charge" or responsibility that it needs to address. For example, as a group, the catechists are responsible for the formal catechesis of the adults, children, and youth of the parish. While it might, at times, be easy to lose track of the larger responsibility in the details of class lists, the session themes for adults, and grade level liturgies, nonetheless, to be a catechist is to be a participant in this larger responsibility. So each group within the parish has a particular role to play in the life of the community, which it accomplishes with greater or lesser success. Furthermore, each of these groups participates in the larger mission of the parish, which is to be and become an ever more effective agent of evangelization.

COMMUNITIES OF PRACTICE

A parish is composed of a number of small groups through which the work of the parish is accomplished. The groups meet with some regularity to address specific tasks that are part of their general charge or responsibility, which is itself part of the larger mission of the parish. Each of these groups can be perceived as a *community of practice* (CoP),[2] and the activities or practices in which they engage as well as the way they engage in these practices serve as an essential component of parish-wide, lifelong growth in faith.

To see each of these various groups and committees as a "community of practice" necessitates looking beyond its specific tasks or goals and examining its inner cohesion and formative potential. Not every group that gathers within the parish is or needs to be a CoP. The group of seven or eight people who get together to give the church building a good cleaning or to decorate for the Holy Week liturgies is not necessarily a CoP nor is the group of parents whose children are preparing for first sacraments and who meets two or three times over the course of the year. A community of practice can be described as *a sustained gathering of people whose interactions are marked by mutual engagement around a shared enterprise with a common repertoire, and where the collective learning involved in thriving as a community leads to practices that enhance the members' identity and further the group's goals.*

How is the term *practice* understood here? To speak of a CoP is to make reference to a sustained gathering of practitioners. The focus here is not first on the activities or the way things are done, the "practices" of a particular group of practitioners, though clearly communities of practice, have practices through which the group's goal are achieved. But when speaking of communities of practice, the reference is to a larger concept, the larger generative idea around which the community is gathered.

When we speak of a law or a medical practice, we refer to the gathering of people who engage in the endeavors of law or medicine, respectively; they are practitioners of law or medicine. In a similar way, when we speak of communities of practice, we are referring to a gathering of practitioners. The catechists form a CoP around being practitioners of catechesis; the RCIA team forms a community of practitioners in the work of initiation. *Practice* here refers to the broad endeavor within which our activities and experiences are meaningful.[3]

In addition to looking at communities of practice made up of practitioners of a particular set of practices that contribute to the end or goal, such as catechesis or initiation, we also consider the practices of a particular group of practitioners, through which a community achieves its goals. As was noted earlier, there are many activities that happen across parish communities of practice— gathering, welcoming new members, discussing agenda items, offering support and encouragement, and so on. How those activities are approached is an important part of our conversation and will be examined more closely in subsequent chapters.

Three elements constitute these communities of practice or groups of practitioners: shared enterprise, mutual engagement, and common repertoire.[4] As we now analyze them separately, their essential interconnection is evident.

Shared Enterprise

Communities do not develop in theory; they evolve in response to a particular focus of interest or a specific goal: the members of the RCIA team, for example, gather to enhance their ability to share faith with potential new members of the wider faith community and to help form the candidates and catechumens in the Catholic faith; several youth ministers from neighboring parishes gather regularly because of their dedication to their work with youth and to their own faith lives, and a group of parents of young children gather monthly for conversation and support with a particular interest in strengthening the faith life of their children and families. Each of these groups—or communities—is rooted in a shared enterprise, a common endeavor to which the members are committed.

The shared enterprise is an essential component of a CoP and serves as the basis for membership in the community. The CoP is made up of and shaped by those committed to this common endeavor. The breadth of this shared enterprise can sometimes be missed in the day-to-day workings of parish life. For example, the parish catechetical leader might ask someone to be a catechist for the third graders, emphasizing that particular task and the commitment that it involves. But when viewed from the perspective of a community of practice, the catechist is also being invited to be a member of a community of catechists who have the shared enterprise of contributing to the faith formation of all the members of the parish community. At some level, the catechist is being called to situate his or her ministry within the wider context of this shared enterprise.

One further point, if the third-grade catechist has little or no interaction with other catechists or with those engaged in catechesis with adults, it would be challenging for the catechist to see the specific work with the third graders as part of something bigger— as part of the shared enterprise of the practitioners of catechesis for St. Odo the Good. In other words, without the expectation that a potential catechist would also be engaged at some level with the community of catechists, it would be difficult to see the group of parish catechists as a community of practice.

The shared enterprise defines the scope and focus on the work of the members of the community; it delineates the group's range of responsibility. The community develops as a function of the participation of the members in this shared enterprise.

At the same time that the community develops in light of the shared enterprise, the shape of that enterprise is defined by the members of the community. The nature and direction of the enterprise only becomes clear in the doing. Consider, for example, the RCIA team at St. Odo the Good. At some level, the enterprise to which they are committed is one that is shared by most RCIA teams: invite those who are interested in joining the Catholic Church to an extended conversation where questions are addressed, faith is shared, and the core teachings of the church are made accessible. But the way that shared enterprise is given expression is determined by the actual involvement of the team members in the common task. The understanding of the goal of each session, the integration of prayer and reflection on scripture, the particular resources that are used, the approach to leadership, and the connection with the wider parish, all take shape in actually doing the shared enterprise. So, while the enterprise may be defined to some degree from outside the community and may be understood only in light of the broader system of which it is a part, its shape and expression result from the mutual engagement of the members. The scope and limits of the shared enterprise of a particular CoP is a dynamic reality formed and reformed in the doing of the work.

To speak of a community's shared enterprise is to refer to more than simply a group's goal. Through the process of defining and living out the shared enterprise, a sense of accountability is fostered. Each member is accountable toward the shared enterprise and, through that, toward the group.

While establishing a committee and defining its goals and processes might be necessary to the functioning of a parish, its potential as a CoP rests in the commitment that members give to the shared endeavor. This commitment is strengthened when the members are able to define the shared enterprise in light of their own interests and passions.[5]

There are inherent challenges in the dynamic nature of the shared enterprise. Since the shared enterprise is not a static reality but one that is being understood afresh as the members of the community give expression to the work in the here and now, it is possible that not everyone will agree with the direction in which the shared enterprise is evolving. For example, a changing sense of the committee's role has moved the shared enterprise of the social justice committee from an emphasis on being involved in direct service to a concern for providing opportunities for the wider parish community to be involved in action for justice. Or it seems that the shared enterprise of the parish book club has shifted from a focus on discussing a different book each month to simply an opportunity to socialize over dessert and coffee. On the one hand, these shifts may be brought about by the addition of new members who bring new interests and emphases that can shape the shared enterprise in a new direction. On the other hand, the shifting nature of the shared enterprise may be traced not so much to the members as to forces outside the CoP itself. A new director of religious education is hired with the directive to emphasize the faith formation of the adults within the parish; this might well have a significant impact on the nature of the shared enterprise of the faith formation committee. In the final analysis, the dynamic nature of the shared enterprise points to the necessity for careful attention to the process of describing the shared enterprise of a community, particularly during times of change, of significant decision making, and of the introduction of new members. At these moments, being attentive to what we are attempting to be practitioners of is of particular importance.

To ask about "shared enterprise" is to ask, "Why?" What is the reason for the group's coming together? This is a multilayered reality. At one level, the reason may seem self-evident and based on the original rationale of the group's creation: for example, to work with the candidates/catechumens in the RCIA or to improve the outreach to youth or to enhance the faith life of the children and families in the parish. On another level, there may be reasons for members participating that are different from, but one hopes, complementary to, the group's understanding. In addition, the larger organization to which the community belongs understands the reason for the group in a somewhat different way. All of these contribute to the dynamics of the group and the way that the group understands its shared enterprise.

Mutual Engagement

The persons who are invested in the shared enterprise constitute the community. The relationships between and among them and their commitment to the group's enterprise define the boundaries of the community. Again, rather than existing in theory, groups come to expression in light of the membership and their mode of relating as they engage around the shared enterprise.

Through engaging with one another in a way that is reciprocal and respectful, the members of a CoP strengthen the relationships or the fiber of the community and enhance the community's capacity to fulfill its shared endeavor. For example, through mutual engagement, the community constituted by the members of the RCIA team enriches its ability to address and more fully give expression to its shared enterprise. The members come to know one another and the endeavor that they are about more and more clearly. Through this mutual engagement, each of the members comes to appreciate the gifts and strengths of the others, learns who they can go to for advice and suggestions, and recognizes their own contribution to the group and its work.

While mutual engagement is used to describe the manner of interaction among the group members, this should not be reduced to a facile "getting along." There are a variety of differences among the members of a CoP, differences that are important to the vitality and effectiveness of the group's enacting its shared enterprise. Members belong to the group in different ways and express that belonging in various modes of engagement.[6]

For example, a distinction can be made between those who focus on the internal life of the CoP and those whose core concern is more external. For those focusing on the internal dynamics of the community, the shared enterprise of the group and its ongoing shape and formation is central. The work of engagement here focuses on the shared activities of the group, the history of shared experiences, and the interpersonal relationships among the members. Maintaining the group's membership and boundaries is important to this mode of engagement.

On the other hand, for some members and in some circumstances, the focus may be on the relationship between the CoP and other communities or the wider context within which the CoP is situated. Here the interest rests in the cross-boundary relationships. Identifying and optimizing the relationship with those communities that have a similar shared enterprise (the liturgy committee and the choir, perhaps); recognizing and strengthening the connection between the tasks of this particular CoP and the goals of the larger community, institution, or constellation of communities of which it is a part (the stewardship committee in relationship to a parish's pastoral plan, for example); naming and sharing elements of the community's repertoire that might be useful to another CoP (adult learning principles shared between the adult formation leadership group and the RCIA): these are the interests of those whose focus is the external relationships of the CoP. These members act as agents between the CoP and elements of the wider community. Clearly, these two roles—attention to the internal functioning of the CoP and focus on the external relationships—are complementary; no group can survive or thrive without both in play.

To participate in a CoP through mutual engagement is not without its difficulties. At a fundamental level, mutual engagement around a shared enterprise presumes that the goal and direction of the community—its shared enterprise—is, in fact, held in common. It also necessitates that the shared enterprise be the primary basis for engagement. As indicated earlier, there may be different reasons one has for membership in a particular community of practice: one might belong to the choir, for example, for the enjoyment of singing or for a sense of belonging or even for recognition of having a good voice. All of those are valid. But the foundational goal of the choir, which might be expressed as enhancing or complementing the singing of the congregation, needs to be the basis for the mutual engagement. So, while a variety of reasons can shape one's participation in a parish CoP—fellowship, concern for the education of one's children, interest in the life and vitality of the parish, desire to invest time and energy in a worthwhile cause, interest in meeting people with common interests, fun, and good coffee—each member and the community as a whole has to have the shared enterprise as the dominant focus.

This engagement in a shared enterprise is marked by mutuality. Mutuality is characterized by a reciprocal awareness of the strength and contribution each person brings to the enterprise. While recognizing differences in roles and authority across members, the call to mutuality incurs a common accountability to the shared enterprise and openness to the gifts of all.

In considering the "mutual engagement" of a CoP, the fundamental questions addressed are "Who?" "When?" "Where?" While the last two questions—when and where—may be more logistical in nature, the question of who belongs to the CoP and the nature of the relationship is more complex. This is discussed later; suffice it to say here that one's membership in a group shifts over time in relationship to one's roles and one's level of belonging and commitment to the enterprise.

Common Repertoire

Through mutual engagement, the members of a CoP develop all kinds of patterns of interaction. Their schedule of meetings, the general rhythm of their gatherings, the way tasks are accomplished, and the way the community marks its shared identity are all formed through this process of mutual engagement and become part of the community's common repertoire, a repertoire of practices through which the community accomplishes its goals—those words, actions, and objects that explicitly address the shared enterprise of the group. For the RCIA team, these include the Rite book; the Sunday readings; forms and schedules; a phone list of members; the rhythm of the meetings; and jargon such as *catechumenate*, *breaking open the Word*, and *mystagogia*. This repertoire also includes the more implicit elements that constitute the groups mutual engagement: ways of interacting, arrangement of chairs, coffee and treats, stories and inside jokes, as well as patterns of leadership and power. All the modes of interaction and the objects that are created around those modes constitute the common repertoire.

Elements of the common repertoire can be seen as concrete expressions, as reification, of the values and dynamics of the CoP. For example: after a long conversation about the sacraments of initiation, a faith formation committee might introduce a number of initiatives that highlight the interconnection of these sacraments and the connection between those celebrating the sacraments and the wider life of the parish. Baptism could take place at different weekend liturgies throughout the year; slips of paper with the names of those preparing for first Eucharist might be distributed at Sunday liturgy with the request that they be remembered in prayer; those preparing for confirmation could help with the first Eucharist retreat and the spaghetti dinner that follows it; those preparing for the baptism of their child could be paired with other parents who had recently had their child baptized for support and encouragement; those preparing for confirmation might be presented as candidates for the sacrament at the youth Mass on Sunday night. Each of these activities becomes a part of the repertoire of the faith formation committee and of the parish as a whole. These practices become the way in which the community gives expression to the essence of the shared enterprise and mutual engagement. They are manifestations or symbols of what the CoP values and recognizes as central to its work and responsibility.

So, "common repertoire" refers to those actions and artifacts, those expressions and experiences, that convey the meaning and intention of the CoP's shared enterprise. Through the common repertorie, the CoP gives expression to and realizes its goals and values. The challenge, however, comes when the action or artifact no longer contributes to the shared enterprise either because the shared enterprise has changed or because the effective power of the element of the common repertoire no longer applies.

For example, a parish moves from a child-based program of religious education to one that is lifelong and parish-wide. But the registration form and the system of fees is still based on the prior model—cost per child; this works against the new, shared enterprise of the community. Or, another example: Those involved in formation for confirmation have placed value on the participants being involved in service for justice as a component of their formation. And yet the process has lapsed into little more than a task that the participants have to complete in the preparation process. This action no longer has the power to convey the value for which it was intended.

To look at the common repertoire, one asks "How?" How is the shared enterprise addressed by the mutual engagement of this community? What are the actions, forms, and ways of doing things that define this community and further the community's goals?

Return to the definition given earlier of a CoP: *a sustained gathering of people whose interactions are marked by mutual engagement around a shared enterprise with a common repertoire, and where the collective learning involved in thriving as a community leads to practices that enhance the members' identity and further the group's goals.* The first three elements—shared endeavor, mutual engagement, and common repertoire—describe the characteristics of a CoP, in other words, what makes a group of people into a CoP.

In light of the discussion thus far, there are several elements that indicate that a CoP has been formed. These include sustained relationships, common ways of engaging in tasks, general consensus on who belongs, shared stories and jokes, common vocabulary and ways of expressing complex ideas, agreed upon values, and recognition of the strengths and gifts of the members.[7]

Conversation and Reflection

1. Select a couple of groups that function well in your parish. Think about them in terms of shared enterprise, mutual engagement, and common repertoire. How does this help you think about these groups and the way they work? What makes these groups effective?

2. Think about a group that is less effective. How might these categories help to clarify where their problems might arise? In what ways might this be helpful for improving or strengthening the effectiveness of the group? What do you see as some of the variables that make this group less effective?

3. Name some groups to which you belong. How might these three categories—shared enterprise, mutual engagement, and common repertoire—help you understand the dynamics of the group better and think about your participation?

LEARNING IN THE COMMUNITY OF PRACTICE

The second half of the definition of communities of practice makes reference to the impact of learning within the CoP: *where the collective learning involved in thriving as a community leads to practices that enhance the members' identity and further the group goals.* Learning takes on some specific characteristics when situated within communities of practice.

Maria is a new member of the advisory team for St. Odo the Good's youth ministry. She brings good insights and ideas: she is the parent of two young adult children and was active in youth ministry in her prior parish. At the same time, she has a good deal to learn as she becomes a member of this CoP: What does youth ministry mean to this group? How do the members relate to one another? Who knows how to fix the copier when it gets jammed? What are the relationships of authority and power within the group? What are the "war stories" of the group—great achievements and less than successful endeavors?[8] Who has a key to the parish center? In the process of becoming a member of the youth ministry advisory team, the newcomer is "learning the ropes"; she is engaged in what Jean Lave and Etienne Wenger refer to as "legitimate peripheral participation."[9]

Legitimate peripheral participation refers to the engagement that new members have with a CoP. It is "legitimate" in that they *are* members; they do belong. And it is "peripheral" in that they are at the beginning level of connectedness and have a minor involvement in determining the shared enterprise, in shaping the mutual engagement, and in defining the common repertoire. For Maria, the new member of the youth advisory team, engagement in these modes of participation is at first minimal. Entry into a CoP necessitates that newcomers gain knowledge and skills in order to move toward fuller participation in the community.[10] The new-comer to the youth ministry advisory team becomes increasingly comfortable and effective in her new role as she learns about the group both explicitly—perhaps reading over the parish youth ministry handbook or reviewing past years' programs—and implicitly—simply by participating in the team's meetings and work. The learning that takes place, constitutive to legitimate peripheral participation, is a *situated learning.*

In describing situated learning, Hansman holds "that people learn as they interact with and within communities of practice, gaining understanding while participating and shaping its history, assumptions, cultural values and rules."[11] This contrasts with the way learning happens in a school setting where knowledge is separated from the situation in which the knowledge is put to use. Knowledge is seen as a free-standing item, understandable outside of the lived context. Even in classroom settings where efforts are made to apply the knowledge to experience, it can often seem contrived or artificial. It lacks the "authentic" nature of genuine practice.[12] Learning within a CoP, on the other hand, is not a separate activity but one that takes place in and through participation in the life and dynamics of the community. The new members—and indeed, all members—learn about how to live more fully as contributing agents of the CoP by participating and shaping the shared enterprise, the mutual engagement, and the common repertoire of the group. Learning is not a separate activity but integral to membership in the CoP.

An analogy can be drawn between legitimate peripheral participation and apprenticeship.[13] Apprentices learn by doing. Drawing on one of the examples that Lave and Wenger develop, we can examine the experience of an apprentice tailor.[14] When a particular apprentice joins with a master tailor, he is given some of the less complex tasks: ironing the completed garment, hemming, or replacing buttons. Through these practices, he learns about various kinds of fabric and the way they need to be handled. He learns about threads and the different styles of needles for different uses. If he has a question—like how to keep the thread from tangling when hemming a full skirt—he'll ask the master tailor or one of the more advanced apprentices. As he continues in his apprenticeship, he is given more and more complex tailoring tasks until eventually he is given responsibility for his own projects. He also takes on more and more responsibility vis-à-vis the tailoring shop as community of practice: he moves from being at the periphery of the shop to becoming more central to the shared enterprise. Less advanced apprentices look to him for guidance and suggestions; they see in him a role model they can emulate in their own apprenticeship journey. While he is not yet a "master tailor," he has mastered many of the facets of tailoring. In a tailoring shop as community of practice, mastery resides not simply in the master, but increasingly in the apprentices as well.[15]

It is important to note that, in this process, the apprentice tailor is not simply learning information about tailoring; he is learning to *be* a tailor. In his legitimate peripheral participation in the community of tailors, he is introduced to the enterprise of tailoring as perceived and understood by the particular shop; he is familiarized with the relationships between apprentice and master and among apprentices;[16] he becomes accustomed to the tools and rhythms of the life of a tailor. All these things he learns in the practice of being a tailor.

One dimension of legitimate peripheral participation that can get overshadowed in the discussion of apprenticeship is the reciprocity of the relationship between the newcomer and the CoP. While gaining knowledge and skills as a newcomer to St. Odo the Good's youth ministry advisory team, Maria is also having an influence on the CoP. Over time, her membership contributes to the transformation of the team. As she strives to understand the repertoire of the CoP, she asks questions about perspectives or positions that had been unexamined for some time. Or in an attempt to gain information, she makes an inquiry that causes others to ask additional questions that can lead to change. At the same time, Maria brings her own ideas and insights about the nature of the youth ministry enterprise. As she moves into fuller participation, her ideas and insights naturally become part of the community's understanding of its shared enterprise and common repertoire. Maria eventually becomes an "old-timer," who then welcomes and supports the next newcomer to the advisory team.[17]

To draw out the implications of saying that a parish CoP serves as a context for situated learning, we need to return to the earlier discussion of the multilevel nature of the shared enterprise for any parish CoP. At the first level, a community meets to address a particular goal or objective; the youth ministry advisory team meets to plan a retreat day for the peer ministers. At the same time, their shared enterprise is broader than that; it is rooted in the wider parish's expectation; it includes the responsibility for fostering the faith of all the youth of the parish and what they do at this meeting is done in light of that responsibility. From a broader perspective, their shared enterprise is connected to the mission of the parish, which is to be and become an ever more effective evangelizer of the good news of Jesus Christ. So, what is being learned and learned anew in an effective parish CoP is not only how to accomplish the task at hand or how that task is situated within the wider responsibilities of the CoP, but also how to be more effective evangelizers, that is, how to live as Christians in the world.

Just as the apprentice tailor learns to be a tailor by hanging out with other tailors and thus engaging in situated learning, so the Christian learns to be a Christian by hanging out with other Christians. To a large extent, our participation in the life of the parish through a parish CoP puts us in an experience of situated learning in which we more fully know what it means to be a Christian. But, there is intentionality in the tailor's experience as an apprentice; he is not just sitting around with other tailors. He is given increasingly difficult tasks as he moves from legitimate peripheral participation toward a more central role in the community of tailors. Furthermore, a similar intentionality needs to be applied to our parish communities of practice if we want them to be effective situated learning experiences for us as Christians.

IDENTITY AND MEANING

Robert is a lector at St. Odo the Good and has been for quite some time. He is one of a group of eight to ten lectors that meets each Saturday morning for an hour to read and reflect on that weekend's readings. When Robert first joined this group (in the mode of legitimate peripheral participation), he wasn't too sure it was for him. In fact, he was more comfortable reading scripture commentaries on his own than sharing with others how he thought about the readings or the way they might come to expression in his life. Over time, he gained competency in the practices of the group and became more central to its shared enterprise. His engagement with this group—this CoP—has had an impact on how Robert views himself as a lector and as a believer: it has contributed to his *identity*.

As members of a CoP, we have a role in defining the shared enterprise, influencing the mode of engagement, and recognizing and employing the common repertoire. The way the CoP comes to expression is shaped by its members. At the same time, the members are shaped by belonging to the CoP.[18] Our identity is constituted in part by who we are as participants in the various communities of practice. It is the intertwining of our multiple memberships in the communities of practice that shape our lives. We identify with and identify as members of particular communities of practice. Even when Robert is not lectoring, his belonging to the community of lectors[19] is part of his identity; it shapes how he makes meaning of the world around him. He consciously and unconsciously hears the homily on Sunday and the evening news during the week through the perspective gained as a participant in the lectors' CoP.

Who we are and who we become is influenced by the communities of practice of which we are members. The repertoire that we practice within a particular CoP becomes incorporated into the world in which we engage. Participating in the enterprise that is at the heart of the CoP among the lectors has given Robert new knowledge, skills, and tools in understanding perspectives and ideas that are different from his own. The repertoire that he has mastered within this community has influence beyond his job as a lector. It has an impact on the way he raises his children, goes about his business life, and thinks and acts as a citizen.

One final point about membership and identity: they change over time. The concept of legitimate peripheral participation is predicated on the notion that all members of a CoP are at various levels of full participation. Each person follows a trajectory beginning from peripheral participation and moving in various arcs during their membership. For some, the trajectory is toward the inside of the community, eventually being recognized either formally or informally as leadership. For others, their trajectory is toward the boundaries of the group.[20] Whatever one's trajectory, it shapes the member's role in the group, his or her contribution to the enterprise, and his or her sense of identity within the community and outside it.

Conversation and Reflection

1. Reflect on something you learned recently through a situated learning experience—perhaps a new computer program or how to play tennis or the ins and outs of chess. What made that experience an effective learning experience? Or why was it ineffective? Do you think "legitimate peripheral participant" describes where you were in the process? Why or why not?

2. Reflect on a recent meeting in your pastoral setting. What did you learn, explicitly and implicitly? If you understood this as

a situated learning setting in which you were learning what it means to be a Christian, what do you think you learned?

3. Think about the multiple communities of practice of which you are a participant. Try doing a "mind-mapping" of the various communities and how they interact. Which do you think play the most significant role in forming your identity? Why?

4. Do you think the CoPs in your pastoral setting have the capacity to be places of situated learning so that participants can become more effective evangelizers? Why or why not? What would need to change or what would need to be enhanced to make that possible?

It is clear from our discussion thus far that participation in a CoP plays a role in the learning and identity formation of the members. Not only do we shape the nature of the shared enterprise and the mode of engagement, but through participation, we ourselves are shaped. The perspective expressed and experienced in the CoP shapes our identity and way of being in the world. The skills and knowledge that we gain are played out in other aspects of our lives. Clearly, participation in communities of practice can be formative. We now consider how communities of practice can become faith formative.

Chapter 3

THE WHOLE PARISH

Looking at the groups and committees that shape the life of the parish through the lens of communities of practice (CoP) provides us with practical insights into how groups function and what makes groups effective. At the same time, turning that lens toward the members who make up the CoP gives us insights into the way that persons acquire knowledge and identity within a situated learning setting. We continue the discussion of communities of practice by turning now to the implications of considering the parish as a whole from that perspective.

We begin with a discussion of the parish as a constellation of communities of practice, proposing that the parish has its own form of shared enterprise, mutual engagement, and common repertoire. In light of that, we turn to the larger question of how the communities of practice within a faith community can contribute to the maturing faith of the whole parish. The faith formative role is rooted in the intentionality with which the communities are engaged and sustained.

A CONSTELLATION
OF COMMUNITIES OF PRACTICE

In the last chapter, we looked carefully at what it would mean to conceive of groups and committees within the parish as communities of practice, each with its own shared enterprise, mutual engagement, and common repertoire. But these are not freestanding CoPs; they gain their meaning and the basis for their shared enterprises from their relationship within the parish. In a fundamental way, we can say that a parish is made up of CoPs like a constellation is made up of stars.[1]

How are we to understand communities of practice in terms of a constellation? In his book on communities of practice, Etienne Wenger describes a series of characteristics that could constitute the basis for a constellation of CoPs: "Sharing historical roots; having related enterprises; serving a cause or belonging to an institution; facing similar conditions; having members in common; sharing artifacts; having geographical relations of proximity or interaction; having overlapping styles or discourses; competing for the same resources."[2] As is clear from this list, Wenger understands constellation in very wide terms. From his understanding, for example, all the tenants of an office building could be a constellation of communities of practice. Our use of the concept, however, is more defined: *constellation* refers to an intentional grouping of CoPs whose shared enterprises are related to one another and are recognized as important to all of the member communities.

In the last chapter, we examined the levels of enterprise within which a community participates. As an immediate level, the CoP has a specific task or focus for a particular meeting or session—the leadership team of the youth group is engaging in the task of planning a weekend retreat, for example. This flows from the shared enterprise of the community (to provide spiritual, social, and intellectual opportunities for the youth of the parish), which is itself part of the parish's shared enterprise to be and become an effective agent of evangelization. Therefore, while the choir, for example, has a different shared enterprise, it recognizes the value of the youth group leadership team and is related to it through the common commitment to evangelization. These two groups could be part of the wider parish constellation because they are an intentional grouping of CoPs whose shared enterprises are related to one another and are recognized as important to all of the member communities.

In light of that definition, we can say two things about constellations: First, while the term *constellation* can refer to the umbrella organization or institution to which the CoP belongs, it can be more than that. For example, a social justice committee could be said to belong to the constellation of the parish and to the constellation of social justice committees within the diocese or even social justice committees within faith-based settings in a particular area or region. In each case, being part of the constellation provides a perspective on the work of the committee.

Second, the constellation takes its shape on the basis in which CoPs are grouped together: Is it based on similar conditions or having members in common, for example, all the arts committees of a particular city or region? Is the defining characteristic that the CoPs are all competing for limited resources, such as the constellation of staffs from national parks in the United States? Whatever the defining characteristic(s), seeing the CoP from the perspective of its place in the constellation provides a context for understanding its common endeavor. In fact, when seen from the perspective of a constellation, the shared enterprise of each CoP gains depth and complexity. We saw that to be the case for CoPs within a parish.

While each CoP within the constellation of the parish—the RCIA team, the youth ministry advisory board, the liturgy committee—has its own shared enterprise, it also participates in the shared enterprise of the parish: being and becoming a more effective agent of evangelization and shaping its members for that task. Consequently, the "success" of a CoP rests not only in its effectiveness in engaging in its shared enterprise, it is also about addressing the enterprise embodied in the constellation. In the case of a CoP that is part of a parish as constellation, this means that the CoP is responsible for its own shared enterprise and for enhancing the faith life of its members so that they can more effectively proclaim the gospel in action and word.

THE CONTEXT FOR FORMING FAITH

Some of the most task-oriented groups in a parish are the most efficient, attending to their responsibilities with alacrity and competence. But are those necessarily the most effective at inculcating the faith dimension into their endeavors and fostering the faith life of their members? Whether we are talking about the youth ministry advisory board or the finance committee, the RCIA team or the ushers, each group within the parish as constellation is called to integrate into their work the overall mission of the church—to be and become a more effective agent of evangelization. To do that, it is the responsibility of each group, within their area of expertise, to bring into focus the three-fold dimension of our faith—relationship with Jesus, affiliation with the Christian community, and participating in the church's mission. While the social justice committee might be emphasizing the church's mission to the world and the ushers might be focusing on affiliation with the Christian community, in the final analysis, each time a group of adults of the parish gather, there is a call to attend to the growth in faith of the whole parish.

As a constitutive component of the parish constellation, each CoP has the responsibility to enhance the evangelizing capacity of its members; in doing this it serves the shared enterprise of the parish, that is, the mission of the church. We can enhance the faith fostering role of CoPs by articulating and embracing the faith dimension of each of the parish's communities of practice, recognizing the communities of practice as the essential resource in welcoming new members and renewing established members, facilitating effective collaboration between communities of practice within the constellation (and beyond it), and working to engage people's gifts most effectively.

Articulating and Embracing the Faith Dimension of Each of the Parish's Communities of Practice

The finance committee meets monthly at St. Odo the Good parish to discuss expenditures and provide guidance in shaping the yearly budget. If asked what the finance committee does (that is, what is its shared enterprise), most of the members would be pretty clear on its specific tasks as well as on its general role of monitoring the fiscal health of the parish and providing assistance to the pastor in his efforts to keep income and expenditures in positive balance. But perhaps few of them would be articulate about the committee's participation in the wider enterprise of being an evangelizing parish. While many might acknowledge the faith dimension of their committee work, few, if any, would think that this work should or could have an impact on their own faith life. And yet we have seen the rationale for having these communities of practice serve as a context for the faith formation of its members. So where do we begin?

As a foundational step, it is important that the description of the committee's charge makes explicit reference to the evangelizing mission of the parish and that all members recognize serving on the committee as an opportunity to grow in their faith. Working from the parish mission statement, which may itself have to be enhanced to make reference to the place of evangelization in the vision of the parish, it is possible to articulate a narrative that embraces the faith dimension of the committee's work. Once it is part of the committee's agreed-upon description, participants are responsible for addressing the faith dimension and evaluating the committee's own effectiveness at integrating faith development into its work.

A second way to enhance the faith-forming role of a CoP is to incorporate meaningful prayer, time for reflection on and conversation about the Sunday's readings, and retreat evenings into the regular rhythm of the CoP's work.[3] Seeing these as integral to the task of the group, rather than as an "extra," is important; time for prayer and reflection doesn't get set aside or greatly reduced when the CoP is faced with a particularly heavy agenda. Over the course of a year, 20 or 25 percent of the committee's meeting time might be given over to this crucial dimension of its work.

A third approach to highlighting the faith-formative role of the CoPs is to integrate them into the faith life of the parish. At a basic level, this might include the recognition of various committees and groups during Sunday liturgy, as appropriate. Or perhaps a different CoP each week takes responsibility for hosting a simple

Lenten dinner as part of an adult faith formation program. In whatever ways, complex or simple, the communities of practice within a parish can be intentionally connected into the faith life of the parish.

To understand the impact of engaging in these kinds of actions designed to more effectively integrate the faith dimension into the life and work of the CoPs, we need to return to a theme that was explored in the prior chapter: the role of a CoP in forming the identity of its members.

At a fundamental level, our identity is shaped by our engagement in the enterprises of the communities to which we belong.[4] Identity in this context refers to more than simply a sense of self or the ways in which I or others name me—teacher, parent, or citizen. It refers to the way in which I view and interpret reality, the perspective I take on a particular idea, event, or experience. Furthermore, this is rooted in the competencies I gain through my engagement with the enterprises that constitute the communities of practice to which I belong.

For example, as a citizen, I have a certain competency in our form of government. I can speak coherently about the three branches of government that are at work at the national level, for example, and that the congress is divided into two houses. I view the news, the dynamics of an election, and political discourse from this perspective. However, my perspective would be seen as fairly basic and perhaps naïve to someone who was engaged in the CoP of constitutional lawyers. His or her identity, shaped by membership in that CoP, would incorporate a more complex and discriminating view of the news or elections or political discourse because their competencies in understanding the government, which were gained by participation in the CoP, would be deeper and more complex than mine. Consequently, the CoPs to which we belong and the competencies gained through membership influence our identity and the way we understand the world around us.

My identity, the perspective through which I make meaning of the world around me, is situated at the nexus of the competencies gained from participating in the communities of practice with which I engage. As such, my identity is always in process; it is affected by my ongoing engagement with the enterprises of the dominant CoPs.

Therefore, incorporating prayer, reflection, and faith conversations within the CoPs of St. Odo the Good has the impact of member developing a set of competencies that support growth in faith. The identity that a lector takes on by virtue of his or her engagement in a CoP that intentionally reflects on the Sunday's Gospel has an impact beyond the role as lector; it forms the competencies that influence all aspects of the person's life.

What would it look like if each CoP in a parish understood its shared enterprise to include the faith development of its members?

Recognizing the Communities of Practice as the Essential Resource in Welcoming New Members and Renewing Established Members

While we often use the term *parish community*, most of our parishes are simply too large to be communities in any meaningful way. Their size makes mutual engagement across the whole parish impossible; their complexity precludes the possibilities of members being able to grasp, much less participate, in a single shared enterprise. In reality, those who truly "belong" to the parish—those for whom the parish has some element of influence on their faith and how they see the world—belong to some small part of the parish, some CoP. In most parishes, and repeated in many different versions, would be the following story: we went to Mass on Sunday but didn't really feel a part of the parish until our children were of school age and I got involved in religious education; or until I became a member of the social justice committee because of its work with the homeless; or until I joined the choir; or until a friend invited me to join the parish book club and I got really involved in that.

Recognizing the importance of connecting with communities of practice for the formation of identity and for the sense of affiliation with the parish, it is helpful to see these communities of practice as resources for connecting new or renewing members[5] with the life of the parish. Looking more closely at how membership works in a CoP provides insights on how the CoP can serve as an essential resource in welcoming new parish members and renewing established ones.

As noted in the last chapter, new membership in a CoP is characterized by legitimate peripheral participation. It is legitimate in that the new members are in fact members and participate in the shared endeavor, mutual engagement, and common repertoire. But they participate in a peripheral way, that is, they are just entering into a trajectory that will lead them from the margins of the group, where one naturally begins, toward the center.

Taking advantage of the role of CoPs in connecting new and renewing members with the life of the parish begins with the recognition that welcoming new members is essential to the health and vitality of the CoPs. New members bring fresh perspectives and presumptions, raise new questions and concerns, and introduce new resources and gifts. As a new member of the youth advisory board, Maria brings her past experience as a parent and as someone involved in youth ministry in a previous parish. She brings her perspective that might broaden or simply refocus the perspective held by the present members. What seems like a perfectly clear and reasonable policy or approach in the present youth advisory board may come under scrutiny when Maria raises questions about why things are done in a certain way.

The role of new members of a CoP—legitimate peripheral participants—is twofold: to foster continuity and to introduce discontinuity or disruption. By learning and enacting the mode of mutual engagement around the CoP's shared enterprise, the new members affirm and carry on the basic ways of the CoP. Becoming familiar with and competent at using the common repertoire of the group, the new members continue the work of the CoP as it has been received. At the same time, new members introduce new perspectives and approaches; in so doing, they serve a function of discontinuity and disruption. The taken-for-granted way of doing things is challenged, or at least questioned. Over time, if the new members are not marginalized, the mode of doing things (mutual engagement) and the focus of the group's work (shared enterprise) are shifted, sometimes in only minor ways and sometimes significantly.

It is in this tension between continuity and discontinuity that the renewal and vitality of the CoP is situated. Some groups have a structured way of bringing in new members; they are elected or selected to fulfill a certain term. Other groups need to be deliberate about how they encourage new members to join and participate. In either case, the introduction of new members is both affirming and challenging for the established members and the sense of identity of the CoP.

Once we recognize the importance of new members to the vitality of the CoP, being intentional about how the new members are integrated into the group is important. All too often, there is one of two responses to new "recruits" to a group or committee in a parish: either they are brought in and quickly put to work—for example, teaching third-grade faith formation—with the briefest explanation of the practical side of things. Or the welcome is less than generous and no one seems to pay them much attention as they struggle to find a place in the group. In neither case is their experience as legitimate peripheral participants recognized or addressed. Establishing a process by which new members are brought into the CoP, integrated into the ways of the group, and given appropriate tasks and responsibilities is essential.

One model for integrating new members is through a system of mentoring whereby an established member is given the responsibility of accompanying the new member for a specified period of time. The role of the mentor is to show them the ropes, address any questions, tell the stories of the committee's successes and less effective ventures, and generally model what membership in this CoP looks like.[6] This has benefits for both the new member and the one serving as mentor: the new member can quickly gain a sense of the community's tasks, garner insights into the CoP's modes of interaction, and attain a beginner's level of competency with the community's repertoire; the person serving as mentor receives recognition for his or her role as an established member and acknowledgment of learning attained through participation in the CoP. Both members are strengthened in their sense of commitment and belonging to the CoP.

One final point about incorporating new members into a CoP: the number of members in any CoP is finite. A parish needs just so many catechists; a youth advisory board or a parish council can function most effectively with a limited number of members. So for new members to come in, established members need to leave. For those committees that have set terms for the members, this is less of an issue (though the situation of "revolving members" in which people serve the maximum term, go off for a term, and then return to the parish council, for example, raises some questions about the process whereby new members are encouraged and welcomed). This is more challenging in cases where there are no terms and where membership is based on some level of knowledge or expertise—the RCIA team, the choir, or the youth advisory board.

At base, it is important to cultivate a milieu where new members—legitimate peripheral participants—follow trajectories that lead them more deeply into the CoP and then, after a time, enter into trajectories that move them out of a central role in the CoP and perhaps out of the CoP all together. It is essential that established members model this in their own engagement with the CoP and in the way in which leadership takes place. Having a regular rotation of leaders and incorporating models of shared leadership establishes both inward- and outward-moving trajectories.

One way of establishing trajectories that move people out or into other elements of the CoP is to regularly provide opportunity for people to say, "No, thanks." At a regular time each year—the end of the school year for catechists; the end of the liturgical year for lectors, for example—acknowledge each person's contribution to the ministry and invite them to consider signing up for another year. Used in conjunction with a process for discerning gifts,[7] this gives people a set opportunity to move on and consider other ways in which to live out their gifts in service to the church and the world.

What would it mean to think of the communities of practice in your pastoral setting as the first line of welcome for new or renewing members?

Facilitating Effective Collaboration between Communities of Practice within the Constellation (and beyond It)

As part of their formation, the confirmation candidates engage in twenty hours of service within the parish and beyond; the youth advisory board organizes this, often with little connection to the parish social justice committee. The RCIA team usually functions independently with minimal interaction either with the liturgy committee or with those engaged in adult faith formation. The choir doesn't really talk with anyone, leaving the planning and communication to the music director. This is often referred to as a "silo mentality": each unit stands independently, accomplishing its own tasks without reference to other units, some of which are engaged with the same people or in overlapping areas of interest. While all these groups might be effective CoPs, their effectiveness and the energy with which the parish mission is addressed would be enhanced through collaboration and cooperation among the parish CoPs.

The foundation for a renewed sense of collaboration is rooted in an awareness of the collectively held shared enterprise of the parish: to be and become a more effective agent of evangelization. At every opportunity, pastoral staff and parish leadership reaffirm the call to discipleship and to the work of evangelization. Over time, this begins to shape the way in which the parish members see themselves and their place in the church and beyond. Inviting members of the parish's CoPs to regularly reflect on and articulate the way in which their committee, team, or advisory board participates in the parish's shared enterprise contributes to an ethos in which collaboration is valued.

An additional way to enhance collaboration among the parish's CoPs is to highlight the work of a "broker"—someone who provides a connection between CoPs and can introduce some elements of one practice to another to the benefit of both groups.[8] At times, this person is assigned to represent one CoP in another; for example, a member of the pastoral council might be designated to be a member of a specific committee in order to facilitate mutual communication. In other cases, the broker is someone who has membership in two or more CoPs and whose identity is shaped by this multi-membership.

For example, Robert, a lector who participates with a group of other lectors in a weekly reflection on scripture, is also a sixth-grade catechist. At an individual level, he brings the insights and a sense of identity shaped by his engagement with the lectors into his ministry as a catechist. At the same time, he serves as a broker between these two CoPs—the lectors' group and the catechists. At a catechists' meeting, Robert might speak briefly about the approach to scripture that his lector CoP uses in their weekly meetings, sharing the questions that guide their scripture reflection with the catechists and talking about how he adapts these for his sixth graders. At the same time, Robert is able to take insights he gained from the catechists' conversation back to the lector group. Both CoPs are enriched by this type of collaboration.

The formation and fostering of CoPs have the impact of creating boundaries. The group of people who share a common endeavor, a way of relating that is rooted in mutuality, and a shared repertoire of practices, language, and artifacts[9] are naturally distinct and even separate from those who do not share in these perspectives and practices. Members of a CoP develop competencies that are not shared by members of other CoPs; they hold in common elements of their identity and their view of the world. Boundaries between CoPs exist.

The concept of boundaries often has a negative connotation.[10] It can imply exclusion or limitations; one could presume that boundaries lead to a silo mentality where the tasks of the various CoPs are done in isolation from one another. This need not be the case. Healthy boundaries serve as a context for learning and for gaining new perspectives on one's own endeavors and practices.

Healthy boundaries hold a balance between clear definition and porousness. As discussed in the previous chapter, CoPs are established on the basis of a defined common endeavor, commitment to mutual engagement, and a shared repertoire of practices, language, and artifacts. One of the signs of a CoP is the general agreement among the members of who belongs and how the leadership functions, which requires healthy boundaries. Clearly defined boundaries provide members of the CoP with a context within which to examine, expand, and alter the shared enterprise in light of the influence of new members and of expectations from outside the CoP. At the same time, the boundaries need to be porous enough to allow the CoP to gain insight from and be influenced by those outside. It is the balance of these two characteristics—porousness and definition—that make for healthy boundaries and effective CoPs.

A parish, for example, holds an annual celebration of the Epiphany in early January. It is an opportunity for a number of CoPs with overlapping enterprises to work together in creating an event in which the whole parish can participate: the liturgy committee, the choir, the social committee, the parish council, the religious education committee, and others. There are a number of approaches to organizing this collaboration. First, one person or the pastoral staff can have a vision that is then conveyed to the leaders of the various CoPs who then execute "their part" of the event largely in isolation from one another. Second, the leaders of the CoPs could meet and discuss the possible contribution they would like to make to the event; this approach allows for a bit more collaboration and begins to draw on the expertise of each of the CoPs in the process of planning and implementing the celebration. Third, representatives from the various groups could gather for an evening that begins with a reflection on the Gospel reading from the Feast of the Epiphany, during which the participants discuss its meaning and meaningfulness for them. This then moves into a conversation about what the participants hope people will experience during the Epiphany celebration and how the various groups within the parish can contribute to it. The evening closes with coffee and dessert.

Would this final approach be more time consuming? Very probably! And there are challenges to facilitating such an interchange.[11] Participants need to be open to the perspective of others and willing to suspend their own agendas in service to the process of the group. But what might be the advantages? First, it models the way all gatherings in the parish are to unfold, with attention to the faith formation of the participants. Second, each of the participants have the opportunity to listen to and learn from the perspectives that various parish CoPs bring to the conversation. Last, each of those present can return to their own group or committee with greater insight into and appreciation for the point of view of others within the parish. It holds the potential for cross-boundary communication that can only strengthen the vitality of the parish.

Another way to bring the richness of new perspectives into a CoP is by offering opportunities for people to experience some element of the CoP without a full commitment of membership: inviting people to participate in a book club meeting when the topic of the selection coincides with their interests or welcoming people for short-term commitments—being a facilitator for a particular youth retreat or teaching children in the religious education program for a specific unit rather than the whole year. In these ways, people who are not part of a CoP can contribute to its work and share in a peripheral way in its perspective.

What would it mean in your pastoral setting to be intentional about facilitating effective collaboration between communities of practice within the constellation of the parish?

Incorporating a Process by Which to Engage People's Gifts Most Effectively

Not everyone can successfully facilitate conversation with adults; for some, the idea of working with youth is really uninviting;

visiting the sick takes a special kind of person. It is the responsibility of each of us and of the parish as a whole to draw on the God-given strengths and gifts of each person in order to respond most effectively to God's invitation to partnership in the ongoing work of furthering the reign of God. Ideally, within a CoP, the gifts of each member are recognized, appreciated, and supported because, in an effective CoP (again, ideally), each person's gifts contribute to the mutual engagement around the shared enterprise.

Meanwhile, the earlier discussion of CoPs as context for welcoming new and renewing parishioners made clear the contribution that new members make to CoPs within the parish constellation. But, in order for new people to come in, the "old-timers" need to move out. It is important that within the ethos of the CoPs, a dynamic develops that supports people in the process of transitioning out of the committee or group and gives people the opportunity to reflect on new ways in which they can live out their baptismal call and participate in the work of evangelization.

While individuals are transitioning into and out of CoPs, the communities themselves are often faced with decisions that shape their direction and ministry into the future: How big do we want the board or committee or group to be? How do we recruit new members? What elements or issues fall under our purview, and where do we need to cooperate with others? How do we communicate with others in the parish? All of these questions in some way point to the fundamental decision of how best to invest limited resources—time, people, finances—to address the shared enterprise of the CoP. The decisions that a CoP makes—both significant and simple—have an impact on the character or nature of the group. Over time, the shared enterprise of the CoP is reshaped in light of decisions that are made; the mode of mutual engagement takes on a new tone; and different practices are added to the common repertoire.

Furthermore, this fundamental decision raises the question: How are individual parishioners and CoPs encouraged to engage in a process of decision making that enhances the best use of each person's gifts? In other words, how is discernment, as an essential spiritual practice, integrated into the life of the parish and the CoPs? While this question is discussed in more detail in chapter 7, let's consider here the ways in which a CoP can be intentional about incorporating a process to engage people's gifts most effectively.

A community begins this process by acknowledging (and celebrating) at every opportunity that the gifts we have are given by God for the good of the community and its capacity to fulfill its mission. Paul's words to the Corinthians make that clear: "Now there are varieties of gifts, but the same Spirit; and there are varieties of services, but the same Lord; and there are varieties of activities, but it is the same God who activates all of them in everyone. To each is given the manifestation of the Spirit for the common good." (1 Cor 12:4–7). Seeing the gifts and talents of each member of a parish or CoP from this point of view invites a response of gratitude for gifts given and a sense of responsibility to employ those gifts in service to the life and mission of the community. A catechist has a gift for working with junior high learners; by providing ways to recognize that gift and set it in the wider context of the mission of evangelization, we enhance that gift. A eucharistic minister is particularly good at visiting those who are homebound, listening to their stories and bringing them news of the parish; by helping the minister to see this as a gift from God enriches her ministry. Ultimately, what permeates the CoP and the parish as a whole is a sense of gratitude—to God for the gifts given to the community, and to those who share their gifts in service to the community and its mission. It is from this stance of gratitude that each person's gifts are deepened.

Not everyone recognizes their own gifts or the ways they can be put to use in the parish. Others might have used their gifts in one context and now wish to find other ways to contribute to the life and mission of the parish, transitioning from one CoP to another. Establishing a process by which people's gifts can be named is an important part of effective leadership of a parish and a central element of establishing dynamic communities of practice. This can be as simple as a person having the opportunity to sit down with someone to talk about what they are good at or what they enjoy doing. Having someone in the parish serve as an "advisor" for people who wish to engage more fully in the life of the parish would be a good starting point. Perhaps the welcoming process for new members of the parish could include time to discern where their gifts might best be engaged in the parish and beyond.

Finally, fostering awareness of the variety of opportunities to share one's gifts with the life of the parish is an essential component for enhancing people's ability to share their gifts effectively. Creatively using a parish website to convey the many ways of engaging with the life of the parish is a good beginning. Being intentional about reaching out with personal invitations when opportunities present themselves is another important approach. In the final analysis, imagining a parish through the lens of communities of practice gives us a way to think about the multiple ways in which people can be engaged in the life and mission of the faith community.

What difference would it make to a parish if people were given the opportunity to examine and name their gifts and use them well?

These four intentional focuses call for a shifting of the shared enterprise of each of the communities of practice from an exclusively pragmatic emphasis, such as planning the next youth retreat, gathering names of those who will run for parish council elections, practicing new songs to sing for Sunday's liturgy. The shift is toward a broader understanding of the shared enterprise to include explicit attention to its faith dimension and to the faith life of the communities' members.

Conversation and Reflection

Attention to these four dimensions can enhance the potential of parish CoPs to be sources of faith formation and development:

- articulating and embracing the faith dimension of the parish's CoPs;

- welcoming new members and renewing established members;

- facilitating effective collaboration between CoPs; and

- working to engage people's gifts most effectively.

1. As you reflect on the CoPs in your pastoral setting, which of these four dimensions are already present and effective? Give examples of how one or more of these dimensions are integrated into a particular CoP.

2. How would integrating these four tasks be a challenge in a particular CoP? How might these challenges be addressed?

3. In what other ways do you see the CoPs in your pastoral setting serving as effective sources of enhancing the faith of their members?

These past two chapters examined the way in which communities of practice function within a parish or other pastoral setting to further the mission of the church in being and becoming a more effective agent of evangelization. To accomplish this, CoPs need to attend to their specific responsibility but also to include the faith formation of their members. In the following chapters, we consider the characteristics and practices that make this work possible.

Part Two

INTRODUCTION

Imagine a dock, secured to the land, and reaching out into a lake. Consider the boards across the dock, neatly arranged, for the most part. Some of them are wider than others; some seem to be made of sturdier planks. But all work together to form a useable dock.

Now, imagine that you're assembling the dock and each of the boards represents one of the multiple communities of practice that constitute the life of the parish: the group of catechists, the youth ministry advisory board, the parish Bible study, the finance committee, the RCIA team, and one representing the parish council. You could add many more boards representing the communities of practice that make up life of your parish, and it would be a long dock.

If you were to take all those boards and lay them out on the water like a dock, what would happen to them? With nothing to hold them together, they would float off in different directions. Some would get tangled in the weed; some of the wider ones would slide over the narrower ones, hiding them completely. Clearly, this would not serve as a very good dock!

In order to make this dock more stable, there needs to be support beams to give the dock solidity. If the planks are the communities of practice of your parish, what do the support boards represent? Let me propose that they are the core concepts on which constellations of communities of practice are built. As we have seen in the first part of this book, these concepts center on the shared endeavor of the parish, which is characterized by the call to be and become more effective agents of catechesis. This is the task of the parish and all its members. So the various elements of evangelization serve as the support boards that hold the planks of communities of prac-tice together.

Let's now attach the planks to the support beams in order to launch the dock. But the dock floats away. It's not a dock; it's a raft. To make a raft into a dock, we need to add pilings, those thick girders that are sunk deep into the floor of the lake and give a cer-tain solidity and stability to the whole structure. These pilings keep the dock anchored and make it possible for it to weather rough storms and heavy surf. The pilings are representative of those dynamics that form the character of the parish and are expressed in each of the communities of practice.

While there are different characteristics that may be central to the life of a particular parish, let's examine four elements or dimensions that permeate the life of an effective parish and are present in each of our communities of practice regardless of the nature of its endeavors: hospitality, conversation, followership, and discernment. The next four chapters examine each of these characteristics and draw out their implications for creating a con-text where lifelong, parish-wide growth in faith is supported and enhanced. The final chapter presents guidance on how this might be introduced in a parish or other pastoral setting.

Chapter 4

HOSPITALITY

*What are the top five ways that your parish community conveys
a sense of hospitality? Which do you think is the most important
one? What are other ways that your faith community expresses
hospitality to both those within the community and those outside?*

Hospitality is a hallmark of a Christian community. The call to
gather as one community in fellowship of love and to welcome the
stranger has been central to the church's identity since its incep-
tion. Throughout the church's history, the theme of hospitality has
come to the forefront, particularly in the context of the work of
religious communities of men and women. In this chapter, we consider the role of hospitality within the communities of practice and
the way in which they can serve to convey the parish's hospitality
to those on the margins or outside the faith community.

In exploring the concept of hospitality, we will begin with our
contemporary usage of the term, proposing that we generally have
an inadequate or minimalist view of hospitality. Second, we examine the scriptures and the place of hospitality in both the Old and
New Testaments, highlighting some key stories in which hospitality and the call for hospitality are prominent. Last, we study the
place of hospitality within the contemporary church, concluding
with a discussion of the pastoral implication of hospitality within
the CoPs.

CONTEMPORARY VIEW OF HOSPITALITY

How do we understand the term *hospitality*, and how is it
experienced in day-to-day life? On Google, the results include a

wide range of references and ideas connected to hospitality—hospitality room, hospitality industry, hospitality committee. There are also hospitality mints, hospitality furniture, hospitality jobs. There are all kinds of connections with hospitality; there is even an Indie pop band named Hospitality.

Considering the use of the term within contemporary culture, it becomes clear that the concept of *hospitality* has in many ways become equated with being nice to one another or being polite. Within the marketplace, it often refers to personalizing a potentially impersonal experience. For example, if I were to call the front desk from my hotel room after checking in, they would often answer the phone with, "Yes, Miss Regan, how can I help you?" In doing this, the hotel attempts to convey an impression of familiarity and relationship that, in most cases, is not really there. This is often true in other contexts as well. Being warmly welcomed by the receptionist in a law firm or a business is designed to convey an attitude of hospitality that, one hopes, reflects positively on the company and the client's experience. In this sense, hospitality is part of the marketing of a product. It is part of a package by which the hotel or business or restaurant attempts to maintain or improve its market share.

Consequently, when we talk about hospitality in a contemporary context, it often connotes comfort and convenience, a personalization of a business transaction. In business, hospitality is also often based on agreement, or it is something that we can buy or pay extra for. Flight attendants offer hospitality to first-class passengers far more than they do to those in the main cabin. In this sense, hospitality becomes commodified—one more element that can be purchased within a consumer culture.

The term is also used on a more personal level. We offer hospitality to friends and family by inviting them to our homes for meals and gatherings or overnight stays. At the parish level, we offer hospitality on Sunday with coffee and doughnuts or at adult education events with the offer of appropriate beverages and treats. While all of these are positive and important gestures, it can be argued that these generally reflect a fairly benign and limited view of hospitality. In these contexts, hospitality is almost always offered to those we know, is almost always reasonable, and most often comes from our own excess rather than from our need.

In his book *Reaching Out: The Three Movements of the Spiritual Life*, Henri Nouwen wrote, "If there is any concept worth restoring to its original depth and evocative potential, it is the concept of hospitality."[1] Scripture and the stories of hospitality serve as a good foundation for such reclaiming.

HOSPITALITY IN SCRIPTURE

Both the Old and New Testaments include many stories that point to the importance of hospitality and its connection with a life of faith. An examination of these stories makes clear some of the key characteristics of hospitality that can be claimed for today's church and seen as an integral element of CoPs in our parishes.

Visitors to Abraham and Sarah

The first story to consider is the visitors to Abraham and Sarah, an account found in Genesis. At this point in the story of Abraham and Sarah, God has established a covenant with Abraham. He has been chosen by God to be the foundation of the Israelite nation; he is told his offspring will be as numerous as the stars in the sky. And yet Sarah has had no children and she is getting on in years. They are successful people with herds of sheep and servants. God has promised Abraham a son, even given him the name Isaac, but no children yet.

> The LORD appeared to Abraham by the oaks of Mamre, as he sat at the entrance of his tent in the heat of the day. He looked up and saw three men standing near him. When he saw them, he ran from the tent entrance to meet them, and bowed down to the ground. He said, "My lord, if I find favor with you, do not pass by your servant. Let a little

water be brought, and wash your feet, and rest yourselves under the tree. Let me bring a little bread, that you may refresh yourselves, and after that you may pass on—since you have come to your servant." So they said, "Do as you have said." And Abraham hastened into the tent to Sarah, and said, "Make ready quickly three measures of choice flour, knead it, and make cakes." Abraham ran to the herd, and took a calf, tender and good, and gave it to the servant, who hastened to prepare it. Then he took curds and milk and the calf that he had prepared, and set it before them; and he stood by them under the tree while they ate.

They said to him, "Where is your wife Sarah?" And he said, "There, in the tent." Then one said, "I will surely return to you in due season, and your wife Sarah shall have a son." And Sarah was listening at the tent entrance behind him. Now Abraham and Sarah were old, advanced in age; it had ceased to be with Sarah after the manner of women. So Sarah laughed to herself, saying, "After I have grown old, and my husband is old, shall I have pleasure?" The LORD said to Abraham, "Why did Sarah laugh, and say, 'Shall I indeed bear a child, now that I am old?' Is anything too wonderful for the LORD? At the set time I will return to you, in due season, and Sarah shall have a son." But Sarah denied, saying, "I did not laugh"; for she was afraid. He said, "Oh yes, you did laugh." (Gen 18:1–15)

When Abraham saw the three strangers approaching, he immediately invited them to stay. In that culture—as nomads in the desert—hospitality was not something that was done to be polite; hospitality was a matter of life and death. Offering hospitality was essential for the sake of survival. So Abraham and Sarah did; they welcomed the strangers, they offered hospitality. While Abraham offered "a little bread," he quickly assembled a full meal with cakes, meat, curds, and milk. There was an extravagance in what Abraham offered to the strangers, an offering of the best of what he had.[2] In that gesture of hospitality, as they welcomed the strangers, they discover that they welcomed angels—messengers from God. They discover that the stranger, who is the messenger of God, is also one who bears gifts.[3] In this story, Sarah finds out that she will have a child and thus begin Abraham's role as the father of many nations.

So, what can be said about hospitality from this story? First, hospitality is essential to Abraham's identity. As desert nomads, hospitality was a way of life. But as the story of the children of Abraham unfolds, this connection between their identity and their responsibility to act with hospitality becomes more and more significant. By the establishment of the Israelite nation, it was seen as incumbent upon the people to be hospitable toward others, particularly the stranger, because of the way in which they had been treated by God. Just as they had been strangers in the land of Egypt and had been in need of hospitality, so the people of God are particularly called to offer hospitality to the stranger. In this regard, Christine Pohl writes that the core narrative of the Israelite nation was their own experience as strangers in a strange land. Not only was that a reminder to them of their dependence on God and the gratitude with which they were to receive God's blessings, but it also kept in the forefront their own ability to identify with others who were strangers themselves.[4] Particular emphasis is placed on welcoming the stranger as the quintessential expression of hospitality in the Old Testament. Just as God offered them hospitality in the desert with manna from heaven and water from rock, so they too must offer hospitality to those in need.

A second insight can be drawn from the story of Abraham and Sarah and their visitors: in welcoming the stranger we welcome God, who is a gracious giver of gifts. This theme is developed several times in the Old Testament; at times, the strangers convey a special calling from God, at other times, much needed provisions. Within the New Testament, the parable of the sheep and the goats, which is discussed below, makes the same point that God is present in the stranger. The Letter to the Hebrews reminds us, "Do not neglect to show hospitality to strangers, for by doing that some have entertained angels without knowing it" (13:2). It is to the New Testament vision of hospitality that we now turn.

The Great Feast

> Someone gave a great dinner and invited many. At the time for the dinner he sent his slave to say to those who had been invited, "Come; for everything is ready now." But they all alike began to make excuses. The first said to him, "I have bought a piece of land, and I must go out and see it; please accept my regrets." Another said, "I have bought five yoke of oxen, and I am going to try them out; please accept my regrets." Another said, "I have just been married, and therefore I cannot come." So the slave returned and reported this to his master. Then the owner of the house became angry and said to his slave, "Go out at once into the streets and lanes of the town and bring in the poor, the crippled, the blind, and the lame." And the slave said, "Sir, what you ordered has been done, and there is still room." Then the master said to the slave, "Go out into the roads and lanes, and compel people to come in, so that my house may be filled. For I tell you, none of those who were invited will taste my dinner." (Luke 14:16–24)

The feast is ready and the guests notified, and one by one they say no. They reject the invitation for something else. When they first got the invitation, perhaps they took it as just that, an invitation; they were excited to go to a great celebration. Then, over time, it switched from being an invitation to being an obligation. It was no longer an invitation to which they would want to respond positively and became more an obligation that they had to balance with many of the other obligations in their lives.

The person who was hosting the banquet was not happy that his invitations had been refused and the celebration would not take place;[5] his response was to tell his servants to go out into the streets and invite everyone—those on the streets or without friends, those on the margins or those with disabilities. Invite everyone you see. And so they did. And when the banquet hall was not yet quite full, they went even further afield and brought in more. Finally, with the banquet hall full, the celebration could begin.

Now, this was an extravagant gesture—welcoming in strangers, those whom no one would invite to a great banquet under any circumstances. It was an extravagant gesture, going against all of the social expectations of the time. The man's neighbors and friends would have considered that an unreasonable thing to do: to give without thought of return, to welcome those on the margins of their social group. And yet, that is the hospitality that we are called to give—beyond what is reasonable. To invite those who are not invited—to offer hospitality to those who are other than us, to those who have no way of repaying us. That is what makes the gesture so extravagant—to give in a way that is unreasonable.

Like all Jesus' parables, this story reveals something about the nature of the reign of God. Telling this story at a dinner hosted by one of the Pharisees, Jesus challenges those who believe that their position is sufficient to gain them access to God's reign.[6] Rather, they must accept the invitation offered through Jesus. In their place, God will invite those who are considered on the margins and outcast—tax collectors, sinners, and Gentiles. This message of God's extravagant hospitality serves as the foundation for our own willingness to offer the same. This is also the kind of hospitality called for in the parable of the sheep and the goats.

The Sheep and the Goats

When the Son of Man comes in his glory, and all the angels with him, then he will sit on the throne of his glory. All the nations will be gathered before him, and he will separate people one from another as a shepherd separates the sheep from the goats, and he will put the sheep at his right hand and the goats at the left. Then the king will say to those at his right hand, "Come, you that are blessed by my Father, inherit the kingdom prepared for you from the foundation of the world; for I was hungry and you gave me food, I was thirsty and you gave me something to drink, I was a stranger and you welcomed me, I was naked and you gave me clothing, I was sick and you took care of me, I was in prison and you visited me." Then the righteous will answer him, "Lord, when was it that we saw you hungry and gave you food, or thirsty and gave you something to drink? And when was it that we saw you a stranger and welcomed you, or naked and gave you clothing? And when was it that we saw you sick or in prison and visited you?" And the king will answer them, "Truly I tell you, just as you did it to one of the least of these who are members of my family, you did it to me." Then he will say to those at his left hand, "You that are accursed, depart from me into the eternal fire prepared for the devil and his angels; for I was hungry and you gave me no food, I was thirsty and you gave me nothing to drink, I was a stranger and you did not welcome me, naked and you did not give me clothing, sick and in prison and you did not visit me." Then they also will answer, "Lord, when was it that we saw you hungry or thirsty or a stranger or naked or sick or in prison, and did not take care of you?" Then he will answer them, "Truly I tell you, just as you did not do it to one of the least of these, you did not do it to me." And these will go away into eternal punishment, but the righteous into eternal life. (Matt 25:31–46)

In terms of our discussion of hospitality, what is important about this story is the identification between those in need and God. In welcoming and offering hospitality to those in need—to the stranger—we are offering hospitality to God. It is the willingness to offer hospitality and to recognize that the other is in need that is the basis of the Christian calling. That is the foundation on which the Christian is judged. The question is not whether they recognized God in the stranger; neither group did. It is whether they recognized the need in the other and responded; in that rests their salvation.

The key point of this story is that hospitality is essential to following Jesus; to being a Christian. In the early church, this was one of the marks of the Christian community—their care for one another, their care for the least among them. According to this Gospel story, that is the basis on which our faith is evaluated—did you care for the other in your life?

These three accounts—and there are many in the Old and New Testaments—present some core characteristics of the Christian understanding of hospitality: First, that in being hospitable, in welcoming the other, particularly the stranger, we are welcoming God. Second, that the Christian understanding of hospitality is extravagant and comes not just from what is reasonable but what might be considered unreasonable. Last, that hospitality is at the heart of the Christian message and, in turn, at the heart of the Christian's life. We are called to be extravagantly hospitable, not only because in offering hospitality we are welcoming God, but also because welcoming the stranger is our responsibility as Christians.

HOSPITALITY AND THE CHRISTIAN LIFE

In her book *Making Room: Recovering Hospitality as a Christian Tradition*, Christine Pohl writes, "Hospitality is not optional for Christians, nor is it limited to those who are specially gifted for it. It is instead, a necessary practice in the community of faith."[7] Hospitality is constitutive of the Christian community and essential to the work of evangelization.

It is possible to make a distinction between entertaining and hospitality. Entertaining is all about the host: how her home looks, who her guests are, what delicious food she is serving or great conversation she is offering. Hospitality is about the guest: who she is, what needs she has, and what giftedness she brings. We can examine the role of hospitality in terms of it being rooted in evangelization, grounded in a sense of gratitude, fostered in the context of mutuality, and directed toward an inclusion of the stranger.

Rooted in Evangelization

At the heart of the mission of the Christian life is the call to be and become ever more effective agents of evangelization. As was examined in chapter 1, *evangelization* can be defined as "bringing the Good News into all the strata of humanity, and through its influence transforming humanity from within and making it new" (*Evangelii Nuntiandi* 18). It is multifaceted in its expression, including witness and proclamation, personal conversion, and social transformation. Essential to this work of evangelization is an attitude or perspective of hospitality.

In the work of "new evangelization," two interconnected dimensions can be named: (1) reaching out to those who have never heard the gospel or those whose connection to the gospel message is tangential to their lives; and (2) renewing the life of the parish that it might more clearly give evidence of the grace and presence of God. Hospitality is a constitutive element of both of these dimensions. In the 2013 encyclical *Evangelii Gaudium*, Pope Francis writes, "All this demands on the part of the evangelizer certain attitudes which foster openness to the message: approachability, readiness for dialogue, patience, a warmth and welcome which is non-judgmental" (165).[8] This is an apt description of someone shaped by a spirit of hospitality.

Rooted in evangelization, hospitality is not something we do; it is a habit of being that flows from a life formed by the gospel and enhances our ability to proclaim that message to others in words and actions. For example, early each October, members of a parish staff send a personalized invitation to celebrate All Souls' Day to the families of those who have celebrated a funeral in the parish over the past year. The card includes the name of the person who died and an invitation to a special liturgy and reception. There is a stamped RSVP card included. For those who are active members of the parish, it is a welcome reminder and an affirmation of their sense of belonging. However, it is also a powerful expression of hospitality and evangelization to the person who is on the margins of the parish and perhaps of the church, the person for whom church is where one goes for Christmas, Easter, weddings, and funerals. It is a real opportunity to invite; to offer hospitality. It is personalized, it responds to a genuine life event that the person has recently experienced, and it expresses care and concern asking nothing in return. It is an expression of the relationship between hospitality and evangelization.

Grounded in a Spirit of Gratitude

Christine Pohl writes, "Hospitality is not first a duty and responsibility; it is first a response of love and gratitude for God's love and welcome to us....Hospitality emerges from a grateful heart."[9] Being in touch with that for which we are grateful serves as the foundation of a generous and even extravagant hospitality. Without the spirit of gratitude, hospitality can easily devolve into either a grudging or a condescending giving.

Like the Israelites of the Old Testament, hospitality originates in our recognition of God's gratuitous hospitality to us. For Christians, hospitality is most authentic when it is built on a sense of gratitude that begins with our recognition of God's great love for us expressed in Jesus Christ. Such gratitude includes recognizing all the things for which we are grateful—the people around us, our gifts and talents, and the beauty of creation. Fostering an attitude of gratitude is the foundation of a habit of hospitality.

A friend tells the story of being asked to be a facilitator for a retreat for the elders of her parish; the theme of the retreat was gratitude. The participants were invited to list ten things for which they were grateful that morning. My friend, who had had a rough morning with kids and cars and arriving late, had a hard time getting past the first few items. When they discussed their lists with a partner, my friend found herself paired with an enthusiastic, animated woman who promptly launched into her list: being alive, sleeping well the night before, being able to visit her husband in the nursing home, his having had a good night, and she went on. All that she had experienced that day was cause for gratitude. In expressing her gratitude, she witnessed to her convictions about the presence of God in her life; she was an effective evangelizer of the gospel message and served as a welcoming spirit to my harried friend.

Fostered in the Context of Mutuality

One of the components of genuine hospitality is a sense of mutuality among those involved. This mutuality is rooted in affirming the importance of seeing the whole person. For those engaged in hospitality, the encounter is more than the roles they play—they are more than host or guest, giver or receiver. They engage as full human beings with hopes and dreams, fears and challenges. It is in engaging in the relationship inherent to hospitality from a perspective of mutuality that the possibility of each person being both giver and receiver is present. It is in this mutuality that we recognize our dependence on the other. As theologian and writer Parker Palmer states, "The stranger is not simply one who needs us. We need the stranger...if we are to know Christ and serve God, in truth and in love."[10]

The foundation of mutuality is shared lives and shared stories. Hospitality rooted in mutuality precludes anonymous hospitality or hospitality offered from a distance. It requires the investment of time and care to become acquainted with the other person, to know their life, hear their stories. This is one of the reasons why hospitality is so often connected with shared meals; it is in that context that stories are told and confidences are shared.

One Saturday a month, our parish offers soup and sandwiches to those who usually go to the soup kitchen downtown. A group of parishioners organized the meal and invited all to join in both serving and having lunch. Sometimes my daughters and I would go to help make sandwiches and serve soup; at other times, we would simply go for lunch. After eating, the adults would sit around the long tables in small groups, while the children were off playing together in the gym, and talk about our children and school activities, local sports, and town politics. Who was guest and who was host? Who gave and who received? Those lines are blurred in the actual action of mutuality at the heart of hospitality. Nouwen writes,

> The paradox of hospitality is that it wants to create emptiness, not a fearful emptiness, but a friendly emptiness where strangers can enter and discover themselves as created free....Hospitality is not a subtle invitation to adopt the life style of the host, but the gift of a chance for the guest to find his own.[11]

While the experience of soup and sandwiches and conversation in the parish school cafeteria is a minor example, that friendly emptiness was being created for all involved.

Directed toward an Inclusion of the Other

A common theme in the scripture stories considered earlier is the connection between hospitality and the inclusion of the other. Whether it is the strangers who visited Abraham and Sarah or the outcasts who were invited to the banquet when those who had been invited turned down the invitation, hospitality moves beyond charity and entertainment to reach out to those who are not included. Feminist theologian Letty Russell defines *hospitality* as "the practice of God's welcome, embodied in our actions as we reach across differences to participate with God in bringing justice and healing to our world in crisis."[12] For her, the central component of hospitality is reaching out to those at the margins, giving preferential attention to their experience, and through this work, changing the structures of power.

When hospitality is about the inclusion of those on the margins, those who are different from the dominant group, the practice of hospitality is more than either charity or entertaining. It is about opening ourselves and our communities to the other and allowing ourselves to be transformed by experiences that differ from our own. This is at the heart of the mutual give-and-take that is essential to hospitality.

As we engage in the work of hospitality, the first questions that need to be asked are "Who is not here? Who is not included?" Asking this first about our faith communities in general sets the agenda for where the practice of hospitality is needed. But we also need to ask it about various ministries, opportunities for leadership, and invitations to participate in decision-making processes. Raising awareness of those on the margins of our communities is an important first step in moving toward being a place of hospitality and welcome.

IMPLICATIONS FOR COMMUNITIES OF PRACTICE

Situated within the life of the parish and having direct contact with its members, CoPs are well-suited to be agents of hospitality. Recognizing that CoPs are fundamental to the expression of the gospel in the parish community and in the world, let us examine four ways in which hospitality can be integrated into their work and practice.

Welcoming New Members

As noted in chapter 3, one of the key dimensions of CoPs is the welcoming of new or renewing parish members into the life of the faith community. Peoples' experiences of belonging and affiliation take place within the smaller groups rather than the parish as a whole. It is within the CoPs that hospitality and welcome is often first experienced by new and renewing members.

How do we welcome new members of a CoP? Communication is important. It is hardly encouraging or welcoming for someone to get no response when they complete the annual "Time and Talent" survey that many parishes use. Perhaps a newcomer, attempting to reach out and get involved, volunteered to help with the annual parish picnic, but the team of people who organize this event have been working together for years and already have the process well organized or possibly don't recognize that they need help or, more importantly, that it is their responsibility to welcome the new member onto their team. As the parish leadership embraces a CoP perspective for the groups that meet and work in the parish, hopefully this parish picnic team of people will also begin to recognize their role in the larger context of parish life and the multiple ways in which they can participate in the parish-wide enterprise of being an evangelizing people.

Welcoming new members, nurturing them in the ways of the particular CoP and the larger parish, and weaving their insights, perspectives, and gifts into the fabric of that CoP's way of engaging are all central to a lived sense of hospitality.

Importance of Communication

Essential to being hospitable is conveying your presence and welcome to the outsider. Reaching out to those outside or on the margins of the parish requires care and attention to how the message is conveyed. How do you communicate your sense of hospitality and welcome to people unfamiliar with what the parish does and offers and with how their gifts might be needed and used? One of the most important venues for this communication in contemporary culture is your parish's web page.

Imagine that you are creating the website not primarily for the members, but for the outsider—for those who don't even necessarily know what they are looking for. Many of the websites of some Christian communities have a tab marked "For the newcomer" or "First time here?" Within those tabs, there is a note of welcome and a series of links: "Are you looking for...Schedule of services? Programs for children? What we offer for youth? Opportunity to grow in faith?" Each of these links connects to brief, clear, and inviting presentations of the programs and offerings of the congregation and an email address if a person needs more information. Such websites are very inviting, very hospitable. Obviously, providing schedules of ministry, dates for classes or programs, lists of contacts for various committees are important for the members and, to some extent, for the newcomer. However, if we begin by asking how inviting this information is to the person who is looking for a home parish, we can foreground that information and have the rest of the information accessible but at a second level.

Of course, this requires an investment of time and money to keep the website up-to-date and inviting. But with hospitality being essential, rather than optional, to the Christian life and social media (including websites, Facebook, Twitter, Pinterest, and so on) being an essential form of welcome, it seems like an important investment.

Welcoming Different Ideas

When we speak about hospitality, not only do we need to ask, "Who is not present here?" We also need to ask, "What ideas or perspectives are not heard here, are not welcome here?" Part of the challenge of welcoming the stranger and offering hospitality to the other is that they bring with them their strange and "other" ideas and perspectives. While this topic is expansive and goes well beyond what we can examine here, it is important to ask about our hospitality to new ideas, to ideas and constructs that differ from our own either personally or communally.[13] Hearing differing ideas or beliefs doesn't threaten one's faith; it strengthens it to the degree that we allow the differing ideas or beliefs to be an opportunity to look more closely at what we believe and why. This type of self-reflection is essential for maturing faith.

It is also within the boundaries of a CoP that new ideas and perspectives need to be welcomed. In chapter 3, we examined the role of the newcomer to a community of practice as a source of both continuity and discontinuity or disruption. In terms of continuity, the newcomer brings new vision and energy that assures the ongoing work of the CoP; in terms of discontinuity, they also bring their past experiences, perspectives, and practices that may or may not correlate with those already in place. The newcomers can be silenced either implicitly or explicitly with "That's not how we do things…" or "We tried that before and it doesn't work here." The vitality and flexibility of the CoP depends upon being receptive to new ideas no matter where they come from. Fostering a sense of openness and hospitality within the CoP as well as in reference to those outside it is essential.

Maintaining Sense of Gracious Hospitality to Others

I recall once entering a church where all the liturgical ministers—lectors, eucharistic ministers, ushers, presider—were standing in a semicircle in the entryway. Unfortunately, they were standing with their backs to the door and talking to one another. This was not overly welcoming! This final way in which hospitality can be integrated into the life of the CoP and of the parish or pastoral setting in general is simply about awareness of our "hospitality quotient" in various settings.

- Is it possible for someone to come into church for Sunday liturgy and sit down without being acknowledged by anyone—even just a nod or a smile?

- Can a new person or family go to the parish center for coffee after Mass and have no one come up and speak to them?

- How is a new (or returning) person coming to a weekly or monthly book club or Bible study or prayer group acknowledged and welcomed?

- How is the mother who comes in early November to register her son or daughter for religious education greeted and treated?

- What is the first question asked of the person calling for information about having their child baptized: "Is it a boy or a girl?" or "Are you registered in the parish?"

There are dozens of other questions like this that a parish can ask as it strives to become more evangelizing by being more hospitable.

CONVERSATION AND REFLECTION

1. In what ways has your understanding of hospitality been confirmed, enhanced, or challenged in light of this chapter? Does this chapter provide new insight into ways in which your parish or pastoral setting presently expresses hospitality? If so, in what way?

2. In what ways has your experience of welcoming the stranger, the "other," which is central to our notion of hospitality, been a positive experience or an experience of God's presence? What have been the challenges involved?

3. Name some ways in which the CoPs in your pastoral setting can be more effectively hospitable to new and renewing members of the parish community as well as to those outside the parish. What are your best next steps?

In many ways, this first characteristic of communities of faith, this call to hospitality, serves as an important foundation for the way in which a CoP gives expression to its shared enterprise. At the same time, all CoPs within a pastoral context—the constellation of CoPs that make up the parish or school—share in the common shared enterprise of being an agent of evangelization.

Again, hospitality serves as the essential underpinning of all such work. In the following chapters, we will see that it is only in the context of hospitality that the other characteristics of communities of practice—conversation, followership, and discernment—can flourish.

Chapter 5

CONVERSATION

*Think of a time when you have been engaged in meaningful
conversation with some friends or with a spouse or family
member or with coworkers. What would you say characterized
the conversation? What made it meaningful? What do you think
a person can do to foster this kind of conversation?*

We have all had meaningful conversations—those interchanges
with a spouse or close friend that move the relationship to a new
level; that interaction with members of a team or committee that
helps to define more clearly the group's shared enterprise; the communication with a colleague that serves as the foundation of a
relationship based on mutuality. These kinds of conversations are
not an everyday occurrence, but when they do take place, they
remind us of the depth and breadth that conversation can attain.
Their role in the formation and functioning of communities of
practice within the parish setting is significant. Not all interactions
within a CoP can be characterized as meaningful conversations,
but they can be a goal toward which we move.

In examining the concept of conversation and its importance
within a parish community of practice, we begin by considering
the experience of conversation in the contemporary context, since
much of what we refer to as conversation might more accurately
be called something else, such as argument, debate, or discussion.
We then consider the role of conversation within the Christian
tradition, looking first at scripture and then contexts within our
recent history in which the call for conversation has been present.
Next we examine contemporary writers on conversation and the
characteristics of meaningful conversation and the means to foster

it. And last, we articulate some of the implications of this concept for communities of practice within the parish.

HAVING A CONVERSATION

In the contemporary context, the term *conversation* indicates a wide variety of experiences. It can refer to the day-to-day inter-changes that people have at home or at work. The desultory chat among parents as they wait to pick up their children at the end of a school day—the weather, the baseball game, the kids' new soccer coach—passes the time but is easily forgotten. In the work context, what is often referred to as "discussion," the exchange of ideas at a meeting, at times sounds more like sequential mono-logues than conversation. Describing this type of engagement, William Isaacs writes, "Often I lie in wait in meetings, like a hunter looking for his prey, ready to spring at the first moment of silence. My gun is loaded with preestablished thoughts, I take aim and fire, the context irrelevant, my bullet and its release all the matter to me."[1] At the same time, political pundits often call for a "national conversation" on a particularly timely topic—healthcare, immi-gration, election finance reform. This has come to refer to every-thing from heated disputes and political bargaining that dominate the news media to the too infrequently reasoned presentation or lecture that attempts to provide a more balanced account of the issues. Perhaps better described with the terms *debate* or *argu-ment*, this type of conversation serves to delineate the sides of an issue, seldom leading to new insights or even a common under-standing of the topic at hand. In her book *The Argument Culture*, Deborah Tanner makes the point that in many spheres in Western culture, particularly the United States' culture, the dominant form of interaction is debate or argument. Tanner writes, "When you are having an argument with someone, your goal is not to listen and understand. Instead you use every tactic you can think of— including distorting what your opponent just said—in order to win the argument."[2] In the final analysis, few minds or hearts are changed by virtue of debate or argument alone.

Consequently, debates, arguments, discussions, and chats may all have the designation "conversation," but for the sake of this chapter, a more focused understanding of the term is helpful and important. More specifically, the focus for this chapter is on "meaningful conversation" by which I mean *the sustained, engaged, and critical interchange between two or more people constituted by active listening and respectful speaking around issues that matter.* The various elements of this definition are examined in more detail later in this chapter.

Clearly, not every interchange that happens within a parish community of practice is, or needs to be, a meaningful conversation. Making the logistical decisions involved in planning a multi-generational Lenten event generally does not necessitate a sustained, engaged, critical interchange, nor does the gathering of lectors who need to practice using the new sound system. At other times, meaningful conversation is exactly what is needed to clarify the community of practice's shared enterprise and enhance the members' mutual engagement. However, meaningful conversation as described here is not easy and comes with high expectations for the participants. In this examination of the context and character-istics of meaningful conversation, it is important to keep in mind that what is being proposed is an ideal toward which CoPs can strive, that is, to have conversations that are more sustained, more engaging, and more critical.

CONVERSATION IN THE TRADITION

An understanding of conversation in the Christian tradition begins with the scriptures as the touchstone for Christian identity and meaning. In the scriptures—both Old and New Testaments—we find a God who is about communication and is made known to human beings in the rich interchange of conversation.[3] The Old Testament is a dialogue between God and the chosen people. From

Abraham through Moses and the great prophets of Israel, God is portrayed as one who initiated the covenant conversation and continued to speak even when the people broke off the conversation by turning away from God's commandments and refusing to trust. Again and again, God invited human beings back into the conversational relationship, an invitation made most explicit and complete in Jesus Christ. "Long ago God spoke to our ancestors in many and various ways by the prophets, but in these last days he has spoken to us by a Son, whom he appointed heir of all things, through whom he also created the worlds" (Heb 1:1–2).

In addition to being God's Word to the world, Jesus entered into life-changing conversation that helped those involved define what was important to them and what they valued. In examining the Gospels, it is clear that Jesus engaged in many such conversations—with the Syrophoenician woman, Nicodemus, and multiple times with the apostles, to name just a few examples. In each case, the focus of the conversation is a topic of significance, one that matters to those involved. Thus was the conversation between Jesus and the rich young man in Mark's Gospel.[4]

Jesus and the Rich Young Man

As [Jesus] was setting out on a journey, a man ran up and knelt before him, and asked him, "Good Teacher, what must I do to inherit eternal life?" Jesus said to him, "Why do you call me good? No one is good but God alone. You know the commandments: 'You shall not murder; You shall not commit adultery; You shall not steal; You shall not bear false witness; You shall not defraud; Honor your father and mother.'" He said to him, "Teacher, I have kept all these since my youth." Jesus, looking at him, loved him and said, "You lack one thing; go, sell what you own, and give the money to the poor, and you will have treasure in heaven; then come, follow me." When he heard this, he was shocked

and went away grieving, for he had many possessions.
(Mark 10:17–22)

Clearly, this conversation is about an issue that matters, a subject about which both parties could be deeply engaged—eternal life! It mattered to the man who "ran up and knelt before [Jesus]," and it clearly mattered to Jesus who took his question and the way he asked it seriously. Meaningful conversations are created around these issues that matter, the generative themes that touch on core elements of human life. At first, Jesus responded to the question with what might have been considered the standard answer: follow the commandments. When the man responded that he had followed these commandments from childhood, Jesus looked at him again with love, perhaps seeing in the man before him a true seeker, a potential disciple. Moving the conversation to a deeper level, Jesus sets out the real challenge of discipleship: to put everything on the line, to set aside accumulated worth, and to follow him. There are risks involved in this conversation that had not been clear in the beginning, the risk inherent to any invitation: the person inviting risks being rejected; the person receiving the invitation risks having to put aside his current perspective to accept something new. And in this case, the man turned down the invitation: "When he heard this, he was shocked and went away grieving, for he had many possessions."

What makes the conversation between the man and Jesus a potentially meaningful conversation are these two elements: (1) that it was about a topic or issue that mattered, and (2) that it challenged the conversation partners to think about what they value. These same elements are present in our next conversation between Jesus and the woman at the well.

Jesus and the Woman at the Well

Now when Jesus learned that the Pharisees had heard, "Jesus is making and baptizing more disciples than John"—

although it was not Jesus himself but his disciples who baptized—he left Judea and started back to Galilee. But he had to go through Samaria. So he came to a Samaritan city called Sychar, near the plot of ground that Jacob had given to his son Joseph. Jacob's well was there, and Jesus, tired out by his journey, was sitting by the well. It was about noon.

A Samaritan woman came to draw water, and Jesus said to her, "Give me a drink." (His disciples had gone to the city to buy food.) The Samaritan woman said to him, "How is it that you, a Jew, ask a drink of me, a woman of Samaria?" (Jews do not share things in common with Samaritans.) Jesus answered her, "If you knew the gift of God, and who it is that is saying to you, 'Give me a drink,' you would have asked him, and he would have given you living water." The woman said to him, "Sir, you have no bucket, and the well is deep. Where do you get that living water? Are you greater than our ancestor Jacob, who gave us the well, and with his sons and his flocks drank from it?" Jesus said to her, "Everyone who drinks of this water will be thirsty again, but those who drink of the water that I will give them will never be thirsty. The water that I will give will become in them a spring of water gushing up to eternal life." The woman said to him, "Sir, give me this water, so that I may never be thirsty or have to keep coming here to draw water."

Jesus said to her, "Go, call your husband, and come back." The woman answered him, "I have no husband." Jesus said to her, "You are right in saying, 'I have no husband'; for you have had five husbands, and the one you have now is not your husband. What you have said is true!" The woman said to him, "Sir, I see that you are a prophet. Our ancestors worshiped on this mountain, but you say that the place where people must worship is in Jerusalem." Jesus said to her, "Woman, believe me, the hour is coming when you will worship the Father neither on this mountain nor in Jerusalem. You worship what you do not know; we worship what we know, for salvation is from the Jews. But the hour is coming, and is now here, when the true worshipers will worship the Father in spirit and truth, for the Father seeks such as these to worship him. God is spirit, and those who worship him must worship in spirit and truth." The woman said to him, "I know that Messiah is coming" (who is called Christ). "When he comes, he will proclaim all things to us." Jesus said to her, "I am he, the one who is speaking to you."

Just then his disciples came. They were astonished that he was speaking with a woman, but no one said, "What do you want?" or, "Why are you speaking with her?" Then the woman left her water jar and went back to the city. She said to the people, "Come and see a man who told me everything I have ever done! He cannot be the Messiah, can he?" They left the city and were on their way to him.

Many Samaritans from that city believed in him because of the woman's testimony, "He told me everything I have ever done." So when the Samaritans came to him, they asked him to stay with them; and he stayed there two days. And many more believed because of his word. They said to the woman, "It is no longer because of what you said that we believe, for we have heard for ourselves, and we know that this is truly the Savior of the world." (John 4:1–30; 39–42)

What a rich conversation! What a life-changing interaction! The woman would never be able to go to the well to draw water without thinking about the day she encountered Jesus. This conversation—one of the longest personal encounters included in the Gospels—highlights one of the characteristics of meaningful conversation: the conversation partners strive to make themselves understood by listening attentively to the other.

Like the previous Gospel story, this conversation is about an issue that mattered—water, this necessity of human life made more significant by the arid environment in which the story is set. And it is about relationships across nationality and gender, an issue raised by the woman in the opening interchange and her response to Jesus' request for water. "How is it that you, a Jew, ask a drink of me, a woman of Samaria?" And, ultimately, it is about believing in the one who can provide "living water" to those who recognize that as their real thirst.

While the opening dialogue is about ordinary water, the conversation moves quickly at Jesus' impetus to being about "living water"[5] as the basis of fulfillment and eternal life and himself as the source of that water. When the woman does not grasp the meaning of his words, Jesus tries to make himself clear by coming at his central point from another perspective, giving her evidence of his identity. This pattern of misunderstanding and clarification, key dynamics in any meaningful conversation,[6] eventually leads the woman to recognize who Jesus is and to proceed to tell others about him.

Throughout the conversation, it is evident that Jesus is aware of the otherness of his conversation partner, the differences in the way in which she perceives reality. He builds from what she knows to introduce new concepts and perspectives. Meaningful conversation is always, at some level, an interchange with the other, requiring conversation partners to engage in the necessary negotiation of position with sensitivity and openness. While the Jews worship in Jerusalem and the Samaritans on their sacred mountain,[7] Jesus argues that both are called to worship in spirit and in truth.

In the opening of the conversation, Jesus proposes a two-part invitation to the woman—that she comes to know who Jesus is and that she ask him for the living water that he offers. Through the weavings of the conversation, the woman responds to both invitations: she recognizes Jesus as Messiah ("Come and see a man who told me everything I have ever done! He cannot be the Messiah, can he?"), and witnesses to others about what he had said. And when she leaves Jesus to go back into town, she leaves her water jug (4:28); perhaps she had left it behind because she had found something of more value—the source of living water promised by Jesus.

From these two stories, we can see tracings of the type of conversation that was at the heart of Jesus' ministry: meaningful conversations, focused on themes that matter to those involved, that invite those engaged to move beyond the surface level of the topic to encounter the possibility of new commitments and perspectives. The questions for us are how can these kinds of conversations be woven into the life of the parish and what are the patterns of interaction within communities of practice?

Conversation in the Contemporary Church

Like many elements of church life, to speak of conversation within the contemporary Roman Catholic Church involves turning to the documents of the Second Vatican Council (1962–65) and the way the Council's insights have come to expression in subsequent years. The Council set the foundation for a shift away from the understanding of the church that had been in play at some level since the time of the Reformation and the Council of Trent (1545–63). This earlier model, with its definite ideas of decision making and communication style, maintained a clear separation between the church that teaches and the church that is taught. Centralized authority rooted in ordination communicated truths and practices to a generally docile laity. There was little need or place for conversation. The basis for the shift away from this model can be found in the dogmatic constitutions promulgated at Vatican II.[8]

Bradford Hinze points to the hopes and challenges of fostering a church that is able to incorporate dialogue into its way of negotiating meaning in a pluralistic context. This requires the development of dialogical skills at all levels of the church and the reform of practices in support of dialogue.[9] For Hinze, an important element of this transition is the ecclesiological foundation on which it is built. This ecclesiology, central to the documents of the

Second Vatican Council, is rooted in a renewed appreciation of the complexity of our understanding of both the humanity and divinity of Jesus Christ, a more developed understanding of the role of the Holy Spirit in the life of the baptized, and an increased awareness of the implications of the relational nature of God in the Trinity.[10]

In the period following the Council, signs of dialogue and the centrality of conversation can be evidenced both at the structural level (for example, the synods and national conferences of bishops, as well as the pastoral councils within the parish) and within a less hierarchical context (including Call to Action, the Catholic Common Ground Initiative, and more recently, Voice of the Faithful). For those who support the move toward conversation, each of these is, to a greater or lesser degree, an expression of the hope that conversation is possible and will be effective in shaping the church into a more dynamic agent of evangelization.

At the same time, the integration of conversation or dialogue into the patterns of church interaction has not been without its critics. Questions arise concerning authority, the meaning of "official" church teaching, and the distinction between the church teaching and the church taught. For some critics, the suspicion is raised that dialogue and conversation are simply a form of dissent and an expression of the attempt at democratization of church structure. For others, the argument is that dialogue and conversation must be shaped within the context of enlightening more clearly the truth revealed.[11]

From the perspective of an ecclesiology rooted in a God who engages in conversation with us as human beings, how do we establish a context, marked by hospitality, where constructive dialogue among all parties can happen?

TOWARD MEANINGFUL CONVERSATION

As noted earlier, *meaningful conversation* was described as the *sustained, engaged,* and *critical interchange* between two or more people constituted by *active listening* and *respectful speaking* around *issues that matter*. By examining the component parts of this description, the nature and process of meaningful conversation becomes clear.

Issues that Matter

All conversations, including those that examine logistical arrangements or that report on the progress of certain projects, for example, ought to incorporate many of the characteristics of meaningful conversations—sustained, engaged, critical, active listening and respectful speaking. However, a defining element of meaningful conversation is the focus: issues that matter. Here, we refer to those topics that have personal import for the people engaged in the conversation; the focus of the conversation relates in some way to the life of those involved. It raises questions about how I live my life, spend my time and resources, raise my children, and engage with my friends. In other words, issues that matter are issues of faith: they ask about how I live a life of faith in my present context. When parents of second graders are in conversation about how to raise children in a consumerist culture or how to help their children deal with bullying, they are just as much talking about faith as when they talk about the significance of the Eucharist to their family.

One way to speak about this is in terms of the conversation's "generative theme." Originating in the writing of Paulo Freire, "generative theme" refers to those epoch-defining themes that touch the core of those engaged in the process of conscientization.[12] Pastoral theologian and religious educator Thomas Groome integrates the notion of generative theme into his approach of shared Christian praxis. "A generative theme" he defines, "is some historical issue—question, value, belief, concept, event, situation, and so on—that is likely to draw participants into active engagement because it has import and meaning for their lives."[13]

The challenge is how to recognize and articulate the generative theme of a given conversation. The liturgy committee, for example, might meet to review and evaluate the parish's celebration of the Triduum. Certainly, asking about the strengths and weaknesses of the liturgies is an approach. But, beginning with a question like, "In reflection on the Triduum celebrations, what aspects had the most positive impact on your own Easter faith?" moves the discussion into the possibility of meaningful conversation. It moves the focus of the interaction from an objective evaluation to a subjective reflection, one that invites the participants to connect their work as members of the liturgy committee with their own faith experience.

Sustained, Engaged, and Critical Interchange

Few meaningful conversations happen in a short period of time, and when they do, it is most often because they are building on past encounters. Meaningful conversations are *sustained* in two ways: they take place for an extended period of time, and they occur at various points across time. The ten-minute period for discussion at the end of a forty-five minute presentation is simply not conducive to meaningful conversation; it is more apt to generate frustration rather than real communication. Time is needed to move into groups; to establish basic connections among the participants or simply "check in" among those who already know one another; to get a sense of the questions or task that is guiding the conversation; to engage in a conversation; and to prepare for whatever feedback system is involved. A group of six to eight with a designated facilitator and three or four well-crafted questions needs a minimum of twenty minutes. More time is needed if a structured feedback process is planned.

In addition to each conversation being sustained in terms of time, each conversation also needs to be sustained over a period of time through multiple opportunities for conversation. If people know that a block of time for small group conversation is a regular part of a meeting, they are apt to come prepared to participate in those opportunities. Knowing that a particular important topic will be discussed over a couple of meetings gives people the incentive to think about their position over time, reflect on what others have said, and consider ways in which their own position might be nuanced and changed. All of these add to the potential for having meaningful conversation about things that matter.

Meaningful conversations are *engaged* interactions. There is hard work in these kinds of conversations in which both the person speaking and the ones listening invest themselves fully in the process. Hans George Gadamer writes, "We say that we 'conduct' a conversation, but the more genuine a conversation is, the less its conduct lies within the will of either partner. Thus genuine conversation is never the one that we wanted to conduct. Rather it is generally more correct to say that we fall into conversation, or even that we become involved in it."[14] To be engaged in a meaningful conversation means allowing the back-and-forth of the interchange to direct the movement, leading all who participate in a direction they might not have chosen.

The third characteristic that marks a meaningful conversation is that it invites participants into *critical* reflection. Critical reflection challenges us to look beyond our taken-for-granted positions or beliefs and ask about the source and outcome of those positions and beliefs. Meaningful conversation engages us not only with the question "What do I think?" but also "Why do I think this way?" and "What are the implications of this way of thinking?"[15] To some extent, for a critical conversation to exist, the other two elements—sustained time and engagement—are necessary. It is only through time and engagement that we are able to move beyond the first level of the conversation and explore the foundation and repercussions of what we think and believe.

Active Listening; Respectful Speaking

At the heart of meaningful conversation is the dynamic relationship between active listening and respectful speaking. Drawing on the work of William Isaacs, we examine four practices that make possible what Isaacs refers to as "generative dialogue," which corresponds in many ways to what is being referred to here as meaningful conversation.[16] The four practices, which are the foundation for active listening and respectful speaking, are listening, respecting, suspending, and voicing.

It might seem odd to begin an examination of what is needed to foster meaningful conversation with the practice of *listening*. Almost always, if we plan ahead for conversations in any way, we think about what we are going to say rather than how we are going to listen. In fact, that may be why many conversations lack depth and significance—few participants are genuinely listening. From Isaacs' perspective, the key to listening is quieting our own inner dialogues; it is the inner commentary that keeps us from fully listening to the person speaking. "To listen is to develop an inner silence."[17] It involves the self-discipline and practice of putting aside our own thoughts and giving full attention to the person speaking.

The second practice in service to meaningful conversation is *respecting*. On one level, respect seems essential to the process of conversation; it calls for a way of engaging and speaking that is respectful of the other. Isaacs takes it a step further by looking carefully at the etymology of the word (from the Latin *respecere*, "to look again"). "Where once we saw one aspect of a person, we look again and realize how much of them we had missed. This second look can let us take in more fully the fact that here before me is a living, breathing being."[18] To respect someone in conversation means recognizing that they are more complex than their particular positions and more complex than we can fully understand. To respect is to recognize and affirm the otherness of those people with whom we are in conversation.

Suspending, the third practice in support of meaningful conversation, invites participants to set aside their own sense of certainty and presume in favor of the person speaking. It challenges the conversation partners to suspend their own point of view in order to more fully understand the perspective of the other. This is not to negate one's own position or deny that a genuine difference exists; it calls the participants to recognize that the position held by the other is authentic. Not only does this involve silencing our thoughts to the cacophony of voices defending our own position or belief, the practice of suspending invites us to recognize that the other is presenting the truth as he or she sees it; is stating reality as he or she lives it.

What can sabotage some conversations is the tendency to categorize people based on their position: he is so conservative; she is a "cafeteria Catholic"; she is stuck in the past; he is too liberal. One expression of suspending is to reframe the way in which we perceive the position and articulations of the other.[19] Instead of thinking of those whose positions or beliefs differ from our own solely in terms of how they differ from us, it is possible to view them in terms of their commitments. What are the commitments they hold that serve as the foundation for their position and the energy with which they embrace and express it? Reframing a response in terms of commitments rather than position or belief alone can be the basis for some common ground.

The final practice is *voicing*. In conversations, we often speak in response to one of these questions: How do I get my point across? How do I refute the other's position? What perspective do I want to defend or uphold? Isaacs invites us to ask another question: "What needs to be expressed now?"[20] To respond to this question and then to name the feelings, thoughts, imaginings, hopes, memories, and so forth that need to be spoken at a particular moment requires active listening that is shaped by the way in which we engage the conversation and the conversation partners with respect, and our ability to suspend our own certainty in service to genuinely hearing the other.

To use one's own voice also requires that we recognize not only what needs to be expressed now, but also the responsibility we have to express it. Finding one's voice and speaking truthfully from that place of self-knowledge is essential to meaningful conversation. At times, what needs to be expressed can be challenging, contrary to authority, or difficult to hear. Voicing in this context takes self-trust and courage, both of which develop with practice as we learn to listen to our own inner convictions.

Listening, respecting, suspending, and voicing are practices that establish a context where meaningful conversation can take place. Combined, they are the foundation for active listening and respectful speaking.

IMPLICATIONS FOR COMMUNITIES OF PRACTICE

A community of practice is built on conversation. It is in conversation that the shared enterprise is defined and realized, the mutual engagement is expressed and experienced, and the common repertoire is developed. To do this effectively and with an intentionality of enhancing the faith life of the members, the conversations need to be meaningful in the way described here. They are most effective when they are sustained, engaged, and critical, and when active listening and responsible speaking are woven together.

As noted earlier, meaningful conversations often do not come naturally to parish committees and groups that are necessarily caught up in the practical elements of planning a particular event, implementing a specific program, or addressing a pressing parish need. However, in order to respond effectively to the broader responsibilities with which they have been charged and ultimately to address the call to contribute to the work of shaping the parish into an ever more effective agent of evangelization, meaningful conversation is an essential component.[21] In order to encourage meaningful conversation, the following suggestions might be taken into account.

Allow for Time

When faced with a packed agenda, the natural instinct is to keep the discussion moving and the decisions coming. This is not always the most efficient or effective. With this dynamic, the following impressions can easily be given: that the decision is a foregone conclusion and that the committee itself has little influence;

that decisions, once made, may come up again and again for yet another discussion and new decision; or, that the various stakeholders do not experience themselves as being part of the process and may not be as supportive of the implementation as hoped. Investment in and commitment to meaningful conversation can mitigate these dynamics.

Meaningful conversation takes time. Sustained conversation with active listening and respectful speaking does not happen in the ten minutes designated on the agenda for discussion of a significant issue. In many cases, the call for meaningful conversation requires rethinking our agenda setting and our meeting schedules. This begins by asking the important question, why are we meeting? On the one hand, there are specific tasks that need to be addressed, perhaps reports that need to be made (though these might be better handled with an email to convey the information), and action that needs to be delegated. But keeping in mind the overarching objective of enhancing the faith life of the members in order that they be more effective evangelizing agents might well have an impact on how we invest our meeting time and resources.

A variety of approaches might be used to get the time needed for meaningful conversation: planning extended meetings once or twice a year to lay the foundation for the kind of meaningful conversation that can be sustained during shorter segments at other meetings; setting aside half an hour for facilitated conversation around a topic of concern at each meeting; and designating some meetings that allow for more extensive conversation while others address immediate tasks. Whichever approach fits the rhythm of a meeting, it is important to set aside the time for meaningful conversation.

Allow for Preparation

People are more able to engage in effective conversation when they have had the opportunity to think about the issue at hand, particularly one that has significance to the shared enterprise of the group. Allow for, and expect, preparation. An important first step is to be clear on the agenda about the focus of the conversation. "Discussion: First Communion" does not convey the topic under consideration. Is it a report of the recent celebration of the sacrament, a discussion of the formation program for parents of those preparing for first Eucharist, or a call to move the date of the celebration to Holy Thursday? Make the point for discussion clear in the agenda. Communicating the various dimensions of the topic to be considered through a brief (one-page) "white paper" is one approach. Having a pre-conversation session through a web-mediated chat space where members can raise questions of clarification and begin examining the scope of the topic can help participants enter the conversation more effectively once in the face-to-face setting. In a way compatible to the dynamics of the group, provide the needed supports so that people can come to the meeting prepared.

Allow for Process

It is challenging to have a meaningful conversation in groups of more than about eight or nine people; each person may not feel free to speak. In addition, the time required with a large group to allow the kind of active listening and respectful speaking may be prohibitive. Dividing into groups of five or six, inviting all the groups to follow an established common process, and including a way to effectively learn from each of the small groups, can contribute to a dynamic where meaningful conversation is possible.

A few standard elements ought to be included in the process that the groups use in their conversation: (1) Invite participants to spend a few minutes "checking in," particularly if the group conversation is the first agenda item. (2) State the amount of time that the groups have for the conversation, and be sure to give a three- to four-minute warning before the time is up. (3) Have each group select a recorder/reporter, and articulate the type of feedback that is being requested: general statements concerning the topics discussed, responses to specific questions, list of items for further large group conversation, for example. (4) Include carefully prepared questions in writing to help the group stay focused on the topic at hand.

Allow for the Work of the Spirit

The shared conviction that the Spirit works through the people of God is the foundation to meaningful conversation in communities of practice within the parish context. By virtue of baptism, each person has been integrated into the life of the Trinity and enriched by the presence of the Spirit. Therefore, providing the time and the context for meaningful conversation sets a framework within which the Spirit can work.

Three dynamics can contribute to this framework. First, as discussed earlier, meaningful conversation is rooted in active listening and respectful speaking. Maintaining basic characteristics of hospitality and mutual respect is essential. Second, as discussed in chapters two and three, it is appropriate to integrate times of prayer into the rhythm of the gatherings of communities of practice. Intentionally being attentive to bracketing extended times of conversation with prayer to the Holy Spirit acknowledges our need for God's presence and guidance. Last, allow for silence. Not every productive moment of a conversation is filled with words.

In the final analysis, sustained, critical conversation is not easy and puts demands for honesty, clarity, and attentiveness on the participants. But it is an essential part of communities of practice and represents a constellation of skills well worth fostering.

CONVERSATION AND REFLECTION

1. To what extent is conversation or dialogue part of the way you think about the church? Talk about experiences of conversation in the church that have been effective expressions of the church's identity and goals. What about those that have been ineffective?

2. Conversations here are described as "sustained, engaged, and critical." Are these characteristics part of your experience of effective conversations? How do you foster these elements in the conversations that take place in your pastoral setting?

3. What are the most significant challenges to effective conversation in your pastoral setting? What are some best next steps to address those challenges?

As this chapter has highlighted, conversation is an essential component of effective communities of practice. It is through conversation that the shared enterprise is made clear, the mutual engagement is manifested, and the shared repertoire is shaped and brought to expression. Establishing a context where these kinds of conversations can happen is an essential task of each CoP.

Chapter 6

FOLLOWERSHIP

*What is your understanding of the relationship between leaders
and followers, between leadership and followership? What
characteristics do you think are essential to being an effective
follower?*

In most contexts—business, industry, education, church—the
focus is on leaders and the role of leadership in the goals and vision
of the organization. Much of the literature in each of these fields
focuses on the role and characteristics of effective leaders. However,
for most of us and for most of our lives, we are more often in the
role of follower than leader, or in some combination of those roles.

A teacher is a leader in the classroom but a follower within
the broader context of the school; a business executive is a leader
with her own division, but a follower to the board of directors.
The director of religious education is a leader in terms of the catechists and parish religious education program, but a follower to
the pastor's vision and to the pastoral council. In each of these
cases, it is not unusual to evaluate how effective the teacher or
executive or DRE is as a leader; that is often the basis on which
they are compensated and promoted. This chapter, however, examines the role of follower and the dynamics of effective followers,
particularly in the context of communities of practice.

After recognizing the often negative connotation that the
concept "follower" has in everyday conversation, this chapter
turns to scripture for some insight into the role of follower, particularly for the Christian. Then, drawing on writings from business, education, and theology, our attention turns to the
characteristics of effective followers and the ways in which they

can be fostered and nurtured, particularly in the context of CoPs. The final section examines the implications of our discussion on the role of followers in determining how a CoP contributes to the faith and vitality of its members and the evangelization mission of the parish.

ARE FOLLOWERS SHEEP?

In contemporary culture, the term *follower* generally has a negative connotation. Few of us want to be thought of as followers; we don't intentionally raise our children to be followers. I've yet to see a bumper sticker that says, "My child was Follower of the Month at St. Odo the Good Junior High." Followers are often thought of as docile, obedient, and passive; not very creative and just following the rules.

Some of the worst images of followers come from those who, when questioned about their actions, reply, "I was just following orders." As the Nuremburg trials after World War II and today's war crime tribunals make clear, "just following orders" can support prejudice, hatred, and even lead to death. Those following orders to shred documents or deceive consumers have at times had disastrous impact.

Even when the focus is not on the more devastating impact of followers, their image is still fairly negative. Followers in television and movies are often either passive "extras" fulfilling the needs of their bosses or clever connivers who get the best of their bosses behind his or her back. Some of the images and roles of followers in media give us a sense of the low regard of this term.

At the same time, our experience of followers often belies those negative connotations. We know of followers who have resisted those in authority, at times to their own detriment. Those who stood up to Nazi aggression during World War II saved lives. Whistle-blowers in government and business have played significant roles in addressing dangerous or deceptive practices. On a more mundane level, it is often followers who come up with time- and energy-saving solutions to everyday activities. While leaders get the credit, it is often the suggestions of followers that inspire new inventions or creative answers.

Over the past twenty years or so, people writing about business and, to a lesser extent education, have begun to recognize the importance of attending to the theory and practice of followers.[1] At first, the focus was on how leaders perceived followers and the role leaders played in enhancing or detracting from followers' effectiveness—followership from the perspective and through the lens of leadership. More recently, research has developed with a focus not on how leaders see followers but on how followers see followers. Consequently, there is recognition that the success or failure of a business or a school or even a parish or congregation cannot be totally explained or based on good or bad leadership. The leader requires followers who are engaged, faithful, and able to express the leader's vision across an array of settings.

We examine some of the insights of the more recent research on followers and followership later in the chapter when we look at the role of followers within communities of practice. But first, we turn to the tradition and consider how those who were followers of Jesus might expand our sense of the follower.

FOLLOWERS IN THE NEW TESTAMENT

To broaden and enhance our understanding of the potential of followers and our perception of our own roles as followers in the various settings of our lives, we begin with the New Testament and the characteristics of followers of Jesus. While the earliest disciples are the quintessential followers of Jesus, those who came after them provide insight into the role of the follower as well.

Engaged Followers

The calling of the disciples and their response to the invitation to "Come, follow me" is present in each of the Gospels.

Leaving nets and family, they respond to the call with alacrity and commitment. This reading from the first chapter of John gives us some insight into the disciples' responses:

> The next day John again was standing with two of his disciples, and as he watched Jesus walk by, he exclaimed, "Look, here is the Lamb of God!" The two disciples heard him say this, and they followed Jesus. When Jesus turned and saw them following, he said to them, "What are you looking for?" They said to him, "Rabbi" (which translated means Teacher), "where are you staying?" He said to them, "Come and see." They came and saw where he was staying, and they remained with him that day. It was about four o'clock in the afternoon. One of the two who heard John speak and followed him was Andrew, Simon Peter's brother. He first found his brother Simon and said to him, "We have found the Messiah" (which is translated Anointed). He brought Simon to Jesus, who looked at him and said, "You are Simon son of John. You are to be called Cephas" (which is translated Peter). (John 1:35–42)

It was enough to have John's word that this was the "Lamb of God" for these first disciples to follow Jesus. When asked what they are looking for by Jesus, their response, "Rabbi, where are you staying?" seems strange, even disappointing. Perhaps that was the first thing that came to mind. Perhaps they were asking Jesus as teacher where he gathered his disciples for instruction.[2] Or perhaps they were lobbying for an invitation to follow him. In any case, an invitation was forthcoming and they followed him and stayed with him for the day.

One of the striking elements of this story is how quickly the disciples—in this case, Andrew—took up the task of spreading the news about Jesus. After spending time with Jesus, Andrew went in search of his brother, Simon, and once he found him said, "We have found the Messiah." It is clear that Simon, soon to be renamed

Peter, took Andrew at his word and followed after him to Jesus. We see a similar exchange later in John's Gospel when Philip goes in search of Nathanael to tell him the news that they had found "him about whom Moses in the law and also the prophets wrote, Jesus son of Joseph from Nazareth" (John 1:45). While Nathanael might have been more reluctant to follow, in the end he too became a believer.

So, not only were the disciples followers, they were *engaged* followers who, once committed, invited others into the experience as well. As followers of Jesus, they embraced who he was and who he could be for them, even if in just a nascent way. And with that sense, they went out, seemingly on their own initiative, to share the news.

Followers into a Way of Life

What is clear in this story from John's Gospel as well as other accounts of the calling of the disciples is that they were not so much followers of ideas or particular teachings as they were followers of a person. In Matthew's Gospel, early in Jesus' ministry, before he has had a chance to articulate his message or present his teachings, his invitations to "Come, follow me" were met with positive responses. It was the person of Jesus they desired to follow. In the Gospels and throughout the New Testament, it is evident that those who followed Jesus were following a way of life, a way of life shaped by Jesus' teachings and formed and expressed by his example.

In many ways, the disciples were being formed into a worldview and style of life that reflected and embodied Jesus' message. The story of the commissioning of the Twelve in Matthew's Gospel illustrates that point:

As you go, proclaim the good news, "The kingdom of heaven has come near." Cure the sick, raise the dead, cleanse the lepers, cast out demons. You received without payment; give without payment. Take no gold, or

113

silver, or copper in your belts, no bag for your journey, or two tunics, or sandals, or a staff; for laborers deserve their food. Whatever town or village you enter, find out who in it is worthy, and stay there until you leave. As you enter the house, greet it. If the house is worthy, let your peace come upon it; but if it is not worthy, let your peace return to you. If anyone will not welcome you or listen to your words, shake off the dust from your feet as you leave that house or town. (Matt 10:7–14)

In this description of sending forth the disciples, Jesus quickly summarizes the message: "The kingdom of heaven is at hand." The details of his instructions are about what it means to live as though the kingdom of heaven is at hand: cure the sick and lame, drive out demons, rely on the hospitality of others, bring peace to those to and with whom one ministers. The disciples were sent to proclaim the gospel, both in the words they proclaimed and in the way of life they embodied. Their actions and attitudes were to reflect what they had learned from Jesus; as followers, they took on the perspective and values expressed in Jesus' words and deeds.

Followers Who Are Sent Forth

One of the places where the mission of Jesus and the tasks of his followers are most clearly articulated is in the farewell discourse in the Gospel of John. As is characteristic of John's Gospel, Jesus gives his disciples a detailed discourse on what it means to follow him (chap. 13—17). These chapters are a rich resource for all who seek what it means to be a follower of Jesus, to be a disciple. While an exploration of all aspects of this section from John is beyond the scope of this study,[3] it is helpful to highlight three core elements of Jesus' commission to his disciples: the call to service, the injunction to love one another, and the invitation to be people of hope and unity. These three elements are woven throughout this section in John.

The call to service. One of the most powerful images in John's Gospel is Jesus washing the feet of the disciples. Although it appears in none of the other Gospels, the description of the event in John and Jesus' discourse about the event points to a theme that is present in other Gospels as well: the fundamental place that service holds for the follower of Jesus. Jesus makes this evident:

> After he had washed their feet, had put on his robe, and had returned to the table, he said to them, "Do you know what I have done to you? You call me Teacher and Lord—and you are right, for that is what I am. So if I, your Lord and Teacher, have washed your feet, you also ought to wash one another's feet. For I have set you an example, that you also should do as I have done to you. Very truly, I tell you, servants are not greater than their master, nor are messengers greater than the one who sent them. If you know these things, you are blessed if you do them." (John 13:12–17)

The strong symbol of Jesus washing the feet of the disciples makes clear that service is central to the life of the follower of Jesus. What Jesus has done for them, they too are to humble themselves in service to others.

Injunction to love one another. This call to be servant-followers finds its foundation in the mutual love the followers have for one another. Rooted in Jesus' prior love for them, this love becomes a distinguishing characteristic by which the followers of Jesus are known. This is the way of life into which the followers of Jesus have been formed.

> I give you a new commandment, that you love one another. Just as I have loved you, you also should love one another. By this everyone will know that you are my disciples, if you have love for one another. (John 13:34–35)

If you keep my commandments, you will abide in my love, just as I have kept my Father's commandments and abide in his love. I have said these things to you so that my joy may be in you, and that your joy may be complete. This is my commandment, that you love one another as I have loved you. (John 15:10–12)

Invitation to be people of hope and unity. A third theme that runs throughout this section of John's Gospel complements this call to love one another. From this love comes hope and unity. Several times during these discourses in John, Jesus gives words of reassurance: of his love for them (13:34), of there being a place for them in God's mansion (14:1–3), and of the promise of the Paraclete or Advocate (16:6–16). Woven into this is the promise of hope and peace: "Peace I leave with you; my peace I give to you. I do not give to you as the world gives. Do not let your hearts be troubled, and do not let them be afraid" (14:27).

Toward the end of the prayer that concludes the farewell discourse in John, we have a summative invocation of Jesus' hope and intention for his followers:

I ask not only on behalf of these, but also on behalf of those who will believe in me through their word, that they may all be one. As you, Father, are in me and I am in you, may they also be in us, so that the world may believe that you have sent me. The glory that you have given me I have given them, so that they may be one, as we are one, I in them and you in me, that they may become completely one, so that the world may know that you have sent me and have loved them even as you have loved me. (John 17:20–23)

Gifted with Jesus' love and the presence of the "Spirit of Truth" (16:13), the followers of Jesus are called to express that through unity, "that they may be one." As we know from the history of the early church as recounted in Acts and lived out across the centuries, unity has not always been easily attained or long sustained; nevertheless, it is at the heart of being a follower of Jesus.

The Gospel accounts give us a rich understanding of what it means to be a follower of Jesus. The followers described here are committed to Jesus and willing to spread the news of his presence and mission to those around them. They became followers not simply in the words and works of Jesus but in the very way of life that Jesus exemplified. And they worked to give expression to that followership through service, mutual love, and a striving for unity.

Clearly, the words *follower* and *disciple* are basically interchangeable in this context. As a Christian, to engage in followership is fundamentally connected to living out one's discipleship. So why not simply use the term *discipleship* and drop the term *followership*, which, as we have already stated, has its own negative connotation? Two reasons: first, for many believers and churchgoers, we already have an image of discipleship that may or may not be as energizing or vitalizing as it could be; using the term *followership* gives us an opportunity to look again at our understanding of what it means to be a follower/disciple of Jesus. Second, within the context of parish life, the majority of people live out their discipleship as followers rather than leaders. The rest of this chapter examines the characteristics of followers and then applies them to what it means to be engaged members of communities of practice within the parish.

BAPTISM: FONT OF FOLLOWERSHIP

Before examining characteristics of followers, in general, and Christian followers within CoPs, in particular, it is important to frame our considerations by analyzing briefly the foundation of discipleship/followership: baptism. It is often helpful to draw on the insights from business and other quarters to explore concepts or constructs that can be helpful in our understanding of ecclesial life. But, as already noted in the introduction of the book, the church is more than a sociological reality. Discipleship runs deeper than followership because it is initiated by baptism and empowered by the Holy Spirit.

One of the main contributions of the Second Vatican Council is the recognition of the common call of all the baptized to discipleship. For those cognizant of the development of the understanding of church during the Second Vatican Council, the rearranging of the chapter schemata for the document on the church (*Lumen Gentium*)[4] from the one proposed by those in the curial offices to the one created at the Council is symbolic of this contribution. Rather than emphasizing the church's authority and juridical structure by having the chapter on the hierarchy precede that of the character of all the church's members as the original outline had proposed, the final version of *Lumen Gentium* examined the nature of the church as mystery and then moved into a discussion of the whole church as people of God.[5] This was followed by the chapter on the laity in which their call through baptism to full participation on the life of the church is considered.

Since the Council more than fifty years ago, perception of the proper role of the laity has fluctuated widely at the various levels of church life. From the understandings of the role of laypersons in the parish or diocesan council to the perception of the laity reflected in papal statements, few suppositions have persisted as clearly as the link between baptism and the laity's right and responsibility to participate in the mission of the church. Few documents have declared it as clearly as the 1995 statement from the United States Conference of Catholic Bishops, *Called and Gifted for the Third Millennium*:

> We consider lay participation in church life at all levels
> a gift of the Holy Spirit, given for the common good.
> Laity can and should exercise responsible participation
> both individually and in groups, not only at the invitation of church leadership but at their own initiative.[6]

It is within the context of the baptismal call for active engagement in the life and mission of the church—service both to the community and to the work of evangelization—that we turn to the literature on followership. Here we raise the question, What does it mean to be an effective, invested, and faithful follower? We then discuss the implications of this for communities of practice.

FOLLOWERSHIP: TYPES AND CHARACTERISTICS

Over the past twenty years or so, growing attention has been given to a better understanding of the role, dynamics, and support of effective followers.[7] The growing tendency to view organizations through the lens of "systems thinking"[8] has led to an increased awareness that all members contribute to the capacity of an organization to survive and thrive. It is not simply the leaders that hold the power to effect change and to give shape to and enact the values of the organization. Thus, the interest in followers.

One of the first books to gain popular attention on this topic was Robert Kelley's *The Power of Followership* (1992), the core concepts of which were anticipated in his earlier article "In Praise of Followers," published in 1988.[9] In those texts, Kelley argues strongly for the necessity of articulating the skills and talents related to followership and then of enhancing the abilities of followers in those areas. He claims that we have failed to do this because of three erroneous presumptions: "(1) that leaders are more important than followers, (2) that following is simply doing what you are told to do, and (3) that followers inevitably draw their energy and aims, even their talent, from the leader."[10]

Followers by Types

One approach regarding followers is to divide them into types based on their behaviors, attitudes, and levels of engagement. Kelley, for example, proposes five types of followers who can be grouped based on the intersection or level of critical thinking and degree of engagement. He sets them out along two intersecting modes of responding. First, followers can be distinguished in terms of their level of critical thinking; they can tend to be highly independent, critical thinkers or dependent, noncritical thinkers. Second, followers can be described in terms of their levels of engagement from passive to active. So, on the one hand, followers may resist engaging in critical thinking, accept directions and positions without question, and simply do what they are told. If they are active in their engagement, Kelley refers to them as *Yes People*; if they tend to be passive, they are *Sheep*. On the other hand, there are followers who are critical thinkers, tend to be independent in their perspectives of reality, and are willing to ask questions. If they are passive, these critical thinkers are best described as *Alienated Followers*; at some point, they became disillusioned or cynical and can have a caustic impact on the organization. The final group of followers, which Kelley refers to as *Effective Followers*, are both critical in their thinking and active in their engagement.[11]

According to Kelley, effective followers are characterized, first, by a capacity for self-management that is expressed in the ability to take on responsibilities and move forward with them independently. In many ways, they see themselves in a relationship of mutuality with the leader and are not overly intimidated by hierarchical structure. Second, effective followers are committed to the organization and the principles and values that it represents.

Typologically, a second more dynamic notion of the movement among the various expressions of followership is reflected in the work of Patsy Baker Blackshear.[12] Rather than dividing followers into types, Blackshear writes of a "Followership Continuum"[13] that describes the stages that a follower might move through as contingent upon their own strengths and attitudes, the circumstances of the job, and the nature of the leader. She names five stages of followership: stage 1: employee; stage 2: committed follower; stage 3: engaged follower; stage 4: effective follower; and stage 5: exemplary follower. Blackshear describes this progression as follows:

The first stage of followership in the workplace begins by becoming an employee, providing work in return for some form of pay. At the committed followership stage, the employee is bound to the mission, idea, organization, or has an internal pledge to an effort or person. At the engaged followership stage, the follower is an active supporter, willing to go above and beyond the routine. The effective follower is capable and dependable. The exemplary follower could easily be the leader. Instead, the exemplary follower sets ego aside and works to support the leader. They lead themselves.[14]

One of the contributions of Blackshear's model is her analysis of the various influences on the ease or difficulty with which people move through these various stages. Her research shows that the same person, who can become locked into lower stages in one job, can excel and be an exemplary follower in a different one. Blackshear looks at three categories that have an impact: internal and personal influences, leadership influences, and system or structural influences.[15]

In the analysis of the Followership Continuum, Blackshear examined both the dynamic that led to high levels of investment, initiative, and participation (that is, a high percentage of exemplary followers) as well as that which contributed to more people at the lower end of the continuum. To some extent, the variables are predictable: those with more followers at the upper stages of the continuum tended to have leadership that was described as providing support and motivation, and to have a positive workspace atmosphere and a sense of teamwork. Those with more followers at the early stages of followership tended to have leaders who were described as incompetent or overly controlling and an atmosphere marked by a lack of communication.[16] While Blackshear's research examines work settings, some of her findings are applicable to our consideration of effective communities of practice within the parish.

Blackshear's model connects well with the concept of legitimate peripheral participation within communities of practice as discussed in chapters 2 and 3. As people come into a CoP, they enter one of several possible trajectories that move them into greater affiliation with the shared enterprise of the community. Clearly, Blackshear's brief description of the movement from entry (Employee) to being an essential element of the life and growth of the organization (Exemplary Follower) is one from the periphery to the center, from receiving directions and the sense of the group from others, to having a more important role in shaping the shared enterprise with others. As discussed later, this movement and the impact of the various influences that Blackshear names has implications for CoPs functioning effectively.

There are other typologies that could be examined,[17] but in the general discussion of followership, all these delineations of types provide three things. First, they provide ways to reflect on the levels and types of engagements of groups of followers or even individual followers (including ourselves) and invite us to ponder why that is the case. Second, they provide ways to reflect on why particular groups or, in this conversation, communities of practice, function well or poorly. In Blackshear's schema, for example, if, on the one hand, a CoP is composed primarily of committed followers, there may be little wonder why the community lacks new vison and energy. If, on the other hand, a CoP consists mostly of effective or exemplary followers, the question regarding the presence of new members might be raised. And, finally, analyzing a group in terms of these schemas provides potential insight into how to improve the formation of followers within and across a parish's CoPs.

Characteristics of Faithful Followers

While the typologies provide a helpful lens through which to consider the roles and levels of engagement of the various followers within a CoP, it is also important to name the characteristics that mark effective followers. Each of the theorists who examined types of followers also named the dominant features particularly of the more effective followers. A review of the various lists indicates some common themes that are worth exploring in more detail. But discussing these salient characteristics, it is important to ask about the specific type of followers we are looking for within a faith-situated community of practice. Here we examine the concept of *faithful followers*.

Like the word *follower*, *faithful follower* can have a somewhat negative and even pejorative connotation. It can make one think of blind obedience, uninformed loyalty, and unquestioning compliance to the expectations of authority. But, like the term *follower*, the word *faithful* can and should be reclaimed.

Earlier in the chapter, we discussed the foundation for followership within the Christian tradition as being rooted in baptism. With baptism comes membership in the church and the responsibility for active participation in the church's mission. Expressed in a variety of ways, this engagement with the task of evangelization requires mature adult faith. From this perspective, being faithful takes on new meaning.

With adult faith, the locus of a person's faithfulness shifts from received teachings, defined identity, and external authority; it shifts toward creating meaning within personally appropriated teaching, self-identity, and internal authority.[18] To claim this shift is to understand faithful followers not as faithful to the church, but faithful in the process of being and becoming the church. These faithful followers are steadfast in their commitment to the always challenging, often uncertain, and at times confrontational process of coming to faith in today's church.[19]

From this understanding of being a faithful follower, and in light of some of the indicators given by those who research followership, we present four key characteristics. Faithful followers take initiative and responsibility, participate in change, serve and challenge the vision and the leader, and take moral action.[20] The discussion of these characteristics is set in the context of examining their implications for communities of practice.

IMPLICATIONS FOR CoPs

Communities of practice in the parish serve as an important context for people to express their baptismal call to discipleship. By participating in parish CoPs, members strive to enhance the faith and vitality of the community and thus strengthen the capacity of both the parish itself and its individual members to be agents of evangelization in the church and in the world. Here, we examine the four characteristics of faithful followers and their implications for parish CoPs.

Before doing so, let us be clear that in speaking of followership within the communities of practice is not to dismiss the role of leaders within CoPs. Whether by role (the parish catechetical leader might be the leader of the community of catechists) or by designation/election (the president of the pastoral council) or by gift and personalities (the person who has the most energy and expertise around a certain project), these leaders play a significant role in the effective functioning of the CoP. However, our focus, here, is on the followers for two reasons. First, the majority of people in a particular community can be designated followers, and yet most of us know by experience how ineffective a community or committee can be if the majority of participants are unengaged, unwilling to take on tasks, or simply wait for the leader to tell them what to do. Second, in some ways, all leaders are also followers, to those to whom they report or to the vision that shapes the CoP and ultimately the parish. In the final analysis, we are all followers of Jesus Christ to whom we owe our final allegiance.

Take Initiative and Responsibility

It seems self-evident that parish leadership would encourage the members of their communities of practice to take initiative and assume responsibility for the effective implementation of the CoP's shared enterprise. Some of the research into types of followers made clear that the level of engagement and investment is dependent not only on the attitude of the follower but is also influenced by the dynamics of the CoP itself. Blackshear names five key elements that organizations can develop in order to foster exemplary followers:

1. Focus on creating organizational stakeholders;

2. Create work cultures where initiative and risk taking are encouraged, rather than ones where full compliance is required;

3. Provide strong leaders, who are fair, respectful, and open;

4. Strive for improvements in two-way communication, information-sharing and feedback systems; and

5. Train individuals to develop and enhance skill levels.[21]

These elements provide helpful points for reflection both for the CoP itself and for parish leadership as it strives to support effective CoPs. Reflecting on the dynamics of the CoP, one can ask about the apparent, though perhaps implicit, presumptions of who is responsible and who is allowed to take the initiative. Similarly, one can ask whose ideas are invited and respected. How welcome are the insights and perspectives of newcomers? More importantly, within the ethos of the CoP, are *they* welcome?

Responsibility for some aspect of a community's work needs to be both taken on by the follower and given over by the group. An effective follower expects that he or she will be responsible for some aspect of the community's work. Establishing a structure that affirms this and follows up with whatever support or encouragement may be necessary is an important aspect of the smooth functioning of the CoP.

Participate in Change

In the United States, if nothing else characterizes the reality of the Roman Catholic Church, it would be "change"! Parishes are being merged, yoked, twinned, consolidated, and closed. A variety of leadership arrangements have been tried, questioned, rejected, and tried again as diocesan officials struggle to address financial and personnel scarcities at both the parish and diocesan levels. And those are just the structural issues. At the level of membership, the change continues. The number of multicultural parishes is expanding and the process of negotiating multicultural and multilinguistic communities is challenging. At the same time, the understanding of what it means to identify as "Catholic" has shifted significantly over the past twenty years, and the impact is being felt at the parish level in the form of Mass attendance, level of financial contributions, and involvement in parish activities.[22] While *change* might not say it all about parish life today, it says a great deal![23]

It is in the midst of change that effective, faithful followers are most needed. In communities of practice within parishes, they can provide insight into the experience of some elements of the parish life; they can give honest feedback to the direction that the CoP or the leadership is taking; and they can encourage the move from small solutions to larger imaginings. At times, everyone—leaders and followers—can have a tendency to minimize the impact of change by making small adjustments: rescheduling the youth group rather than rethinking what the youth group is about; changing the textbook series rather than looking more closely at the overall mission of faith formation within the parish; adding more sessions to the marriage formation program rather than asking how else might the parish support married relationships in general. Followers are called to the important role of being faithful, critical supporters of change.[24]

Support and Challenge the Vision and the Leader

In chapters 2 and 3, we examined the complexity of the shared enterprise that is a foundational element of a community of practice. The shared enterprise defines the scope and focus of the work of the members of the community; it delineates the group's range of responsibility. It is the shared enterprise that expresses the vision of the community. As such, the vision both shapes the group's identity and is shaped by it. It is both specific to each CoP and yet connected to the larger shared enterprise and vision of the parish and the wider church. Furthermore, in the context of followers, it both guides them and is guided by them. It is in this way that followers are called to both support the vision and challenge it as needed.

This task to both support and challenge the vision and the leader is a complex one and requires two significant skill sets among the followers: being able to engage in sustained, critical conversation[25] and being able to disagree. In his book *Plurality and Ambiguity*, theologian David Tracy writes about the rules of conversation that factor in disagreement and conflict:

> Conversation is a game with some hard rules: say only what you mean; say it as accurately as you can; listen to and respect what the other says, however different or other; be willing to correct or defend your opinion if challenged by the conversation partner; be willing to argue if necessary, to confront if demanded, to endure necessary conflict, to change your mind if the evidence suggests it.[26]

Tracy reminds us that to engage in a meaningful conversation is a challenging endeavor that requires us to be attentive to the interchange, responsible in our responses, and open to change. This is essential to a faithful follower willing to challenge the vision and/or the leader.

In reflecting on the role of followers in supporting and challenging the leader, the starting point is that they presume in favor of the leadership.[27] Whether the followers have been involved in the selection of the leader or not (e.g., parish pastors who are assigned by bishops often with minimal consultation), they begin with a commitment to respond to the leader with support and affirmation. Obviously, this doesn't preclude asking hard questions, proposing alternative plans, or even dissenting from a decision that is accepted by the majority in the group. It is important to keep in mind the above description of faithful follower: in this case, it could be argued that the follower isn't faithful to the leader but to the process of interpreting and giving life to the shared vision. At times, this is difficult, perhaps even impossible; that is where the final characteristic comes into play.

Take Moral Action

In examining the importance of effective followers taking a moral stand when necessary, management consultant Ira Chaleff writes, "Moral action is taken with the intention of bringing the actions of the leadership and organization into line with fundamental values that govern decent organizational behavior while preserving the capacity of the organization to fulfill its purpose."[28] This action can range from protest within the organization, to resigning, to engaging in whistle-blowing activities; and the potential types of actions across the spectrum are large indeed. While Chaleff is specifically addressing business and political organizations, many of his insights are applicable to followers within the parish context.

Within the context of parish communities of practice, most of us would seldom find ourselves in a situation that is legally challenging. However, there may be times when decisions that are being made or the way in which decisions are made can be problematic in the sense that they are not in keeping with the values of the group or the wider vision of the parish; at times they can be at odds with the wider church's mission of being an agent of evangelization. At these times, it is important to have clarity about how well our own values correspond with the group's, how seriously the decision influences the group's ability to achieve its shared endeavor, and how significant the results might be on the wider vision of parish and church. In thinking about the best next step, applying the concept of subsidiarity is important: going to one's bishop because of a serious disagreement with the parish catechetical leader disregards this principle. Naming who can be part of the solution and avoiding expanding the levels of involvement beyond the necessary boundaries is an important aspect of taking moral action.

The key to taking moral action as a faithful follower is really the decision-making process; good-intentioned people can disagree on what the best plan of action might be—staying in or leaving a situation, keeping the discussion internal or making it more public, and so on. It is in the decision-making process that the follower makes clear for him- or herself and others the responsibilities of being faithful.

CONVERSATION AND REFLECTION

1. Reflect on your response to the opening question: *What is your understanding of the relationship between leaders and followers, between leadership and followership?* What characteristics are essential to being an effective follower? In what ways have the ideas in this chapter enhanced, confirmed, or challenged your prior understanding?

2. The term *faithful followers* is a challenge since both words— *faithful* and *follower*—have connotations of uncritical passivity. The chapter has been about revitalizing the terms so that they can be used to speak about ways in which adults give expression to their baptismal call within the context of communities of practice. Do you find the term helpful? Why or why not? How else might you speak of the effective participants in parish life?

3. In what ways are followers in your pastoral setting supported and encouraged to enhance their skills and capacities? What else can be done in this vital area?

We conclude this chapter with two quotes from the 1980 document *Called and Gifted*, in which the bishops of the United States articulate four calls that are at the heart of the Christian life:

the call to adulthood, to holiness, to ministry, and to service in the world. Both quotes are drawn from the discussion of the call to adulthood:

> One of the chief characteristics of lay men and women today is their growing sense of being adult members of the Church. Adulthood implies knowledge, experience and awareness, freedom and responsibility, and mutuality in relationships.
>
> ...The adult character of the People of God flows from baptism and confirmation which are the foundation of the Christian life and ministry.[29]

These are apt descriptors of the nature and source of faithful followers, faithful to their baptismal call and to the task of being and becoming a more effective evangelizing church.

Chapter 7

DISCERNMENT

Think about a significant decision you have made. What process was involved in coming to the decision? What roles did other people, reasoning with pro and con lists, gathering information, or prayer play in the decision making? Did you think of that as discernment? Why or why not?

In the past few chapters, we have been examining key dynamics that shape the character of a parish and are expressed in each of the communities of practice. We have looked at hospitality, sustained conversation, and faithful followership. The final characteristic is discernment, which, in many ways, builds on the other dimensions considered thus far. It is through an attitude of discernment that a community of practice as a whole and the members within it come to live in ways that point to and participate in God's action in the world.

We begin with a brief comment on the way in which discernment is used within a secular context, and then examine examples of discernment, both personal and communal, that are in scripture, principally the Acts of the Apostles. The third part considers contemporary writing on discernment with particular attention to the way in which the insights of Ignatius of Loyola are made accessible today. Finally, we draw out the implications for communities of practice.

IS *DISCERNMENT* THE *NEW DECISION*?

The marketing department of a large corporation goes on a weekend retreat to discern this year's ad campaign. A college admissions coach sets out a formula for weighing the various dimensions of each college—location, size, financial aid package, available majors, and so on—to help the high school senior and his parents in their discernment of the best college choice. A parish pastoral council takes a day of prayer and reflection in the process of discerning the next steps in responding to the reality of its increasing multicultural population. In these two examples, discernment is used in distinctly different ways.

Even in the Christian context, the term *discernment* is used in a variety of ways. In many contexts, *discernment* is used simply as a synonym for *decision making*. There is an emphasis on the rational, on gathering data, and on weighing options. While these are certainly part of a discernment process, they don't tell the whole story. As the understanding of discernment unfolds in this chapter, we see that it is more than a process; it is also a gift. It is more than a decision; it is also a way of life. It draws on more than the rational; it is attentive to the extra-rational as well. In its most inclusive sense, we can speak of discernment as a marshaling of the resources of our lives in an attempt to live most authentically in relationship with God, ourselves, and the world around us. Jesuit priest David Lonsdale writes of discernment as "allowing our deepest attitudes, aspirations, values, and relationships to come to the surface, so that it is they which give shape and direction to our choices."[1]

As we examine the dynamics of discernment within the Christian context, let's turn to the scriptures for insight and direction. Although the term *discernment* is not used often, the themes that underpin a discerning way of life are present in the pages of the Old and New Testaments.

DISCERNMENT IN SCRIPTURE

In light of scripture, what can be said about the process of discernment; what do the stories of discernment within the Old and New Testament tell us about this aspect of the Christian life? Here we can refer to two related stories that appear in the Acts of the Apostles: the story of Peter and Cornelius in Acts 10 and the account of the Council of Jerusalem in Acts 15. The first is the story of the discernment of an individual in his relationship to his community and the events of his life; the second tells of a community reaching a common decision that would have ramifications for the nature of the Christian church far into the future.

Peter and Cornelius

Acts 10 tells the story of the interaction between Cornelius and Peter. While different in many ways, these men also hold things in common: both were devout men with prayer being central to their lives, and both men were open to the presence and leading of God. The account begins with the Gentile, Cornelius, having a vision in which God assures him that his prayers have been heard and that Cornelius is to send for Peter, which he does. The next day, as Cornelius's people are nearing Joppa where Peter is staying, Peter is on the roof in prayer, and he also has a vision:

> He saw the heaven opened and something like a large sheet coming down, being lowered to the ground by its four corners. In it were all kinds of four-footed creatures and reptiles and birds of the air. Then he heard a voice saying, "Get up, Peter; kill and eat." But Peter said, "By no means, Lord; for I have never eaten anything that is profane or unclean." The voice said to him again, a second time, "What God has made clean, you must not call profane." This happened three times, and the thing was suddenly taken up to heaven. (Acts 10:11–16)

As Peter reflects on the meaning of this vision, the people sent by Cornelius arrive to ask Peter to come to Cornelius's house. When the visitors told the account of God's message to Cornelius, Peter invited them into his home, not the usual interchange between Gentiles and devout Jews. The next day, they go to Caesarea to see Cornelius; Peter says, "You yourselves know that it is unlawful for a Jew to associate with or to visit a Gentile; but God has shown me that I should not call anyone profane or unclean. So when I was sent for, I came without objection. Now may I ask why you sent for me?" (Acts 10:28–29). Cornelius then tells again the story of the messenger of God appearing to him and commanding him to send for Peter. Hearing the story, Peter affirms Cornelius and responds, "I truly understand that God shows no partiality, but in every nation anyone who fears him and does what is right is acceptable to him" (vv. 34–35). And he begins preaching the gospel to them. Chapter 10 in Acts closes with what must have been an amazing event for Peter and the other believers:

> While Peter was still speaking, the Holy Spirit fell upon all who heard the word. The circumcised believers who had come with Peter were astounded that the gift of the Holy Spirit had been poured out even on the Gentiles, for they heard them speaking in tongues and extolling God. Then Peter said, "Can anyone withhold the water for baptizing these people who have received the Holy Spirit just as we have?" So he ordered them to be baptized in the name of Jesus Christ. Then they invited him to stay for several days. (Acts 10:44–48)

What does this account tell us about the process of discernment? Let me propose four elements. First, discernment begins not with a particular decision to make or with an issue to resolve; it begins with a life marked by prayer. Peter's experience originates in prayer; at midday, he goes up to the roof to pray (Acts 10:9). God's presence is there, but it relies first on prayer to be made manifest. It is within the context of a relationship with God that Peter roots the discernment process that unfolds before him. Second, the element of human trust is important.[2] Peter's vision is odd, but rather than dismiss it as a flight of fancy caused by hunger (10:9), he takes it seriously: "Peter was greatly puzzled about what to make of the vision that he had seen" (10:17).

Third, the process of discernment for Peter incorporated an interrelationship between his religious and cultural tradition and his present experience. It seems as though the vision begins to make sense when he hears about Cornelius's experience with a messenger from God. Peter allows this to be a dynamic relationship, rooted in the tradition but open to new expressions. And, finally, woven into the whole chapter is the role of narrative.[3] Cornelius tells the story of the divine messengers to his servants, who then recount it to Peter. This narrative is at the basis of Peter's willingness to welcome Gentiles into his home and go with them the next day. After hearing Cornelius's story again, Peter retells *the* story, the story of salvation in Jesus Christ.

For Peter, then, discerning God's presence and hope in this situation was rooted in a life of prayer, which was the foundation for a relationship of trust and openness to God's action in his life and the life of others. In addition, discernment takes place at the intersection of tradition and lived experience, in a balance of memory of the past and openness to the future. And it is shaped and given form through narrative, through the stories of individual people and of God's people as they are open to the signs of God's presence. These same themes are present in the way in which the community decision is made at the Council of Jerusalem. We will see echoes of these themes in the discussion of contemporary understandings of discernment later in the chapter.

The Council of Jerusalem

The discernment and action of Peter plays an important role in the discernment process that takes place at what has been referred to as the "Council of Jerusalem."[4] But as the story unfolds in Acts 15, it is Paul's work with the Gentiles that is under question. The question for discernment is this: Should the Gentiles who want to become Christian be required to follow Jewish laws, particularly concerning circumcision and dietary rule? Those on both sides of the question have their valid points and positions. A Jewish elder might say, "I believe that if a Gentile wants to become

Christian, that's fine. But he must first commit himself to honor Jewish traditions and the laws set out by Moses. He must be circumcised. All Gentiles must follow Jewish dietary rules. That only makes sense and that's the way we have been doing it from the beginning. We have followed these laws all our life. We must preserve our traditions and ways. Surely God does not want us to change the law!" Paul, on the other hand, might argue, "I am trying to ask you to see beyond the laws! It is not necessary to circumcise the Gentiles and direct them to observe the Law of Moses. What is important is that they accept Christ. It is Jesus Christ who unites us now. I am begging you to accept the Gentile believers so that I can continue to do my work—to spread the good news of Jesus to everyone who wants to hear it!" Discernment is necessary at the point of conflict between two positive values; in this case, preserving the tradition on the one hand and being open to current experience on the other.

Acts 15 begins with an account of "certain individuals [who] came down from Judea" and said that the Gentiles need to be circumcised and instructed to follow Jewish law. Paul and Barnabas dissented from this and were subsequently sent to Jerusalem to discuss the issue "with the apostles and the elders" (Acts 15:1–2). Once they arrive in Jerusalem, the debate is repeated with some arguing for the need that the Gentiles follow Jewish law and others, particularly Peter, Paul, and Barnabas, telling the stories of God's actions with the Gentiles and the saving work of God through Jesus.[5] After these narrative accounts, James addresses the community gathered. He begins by connecting the current experience of Peter and Paul with the tradition and linking them with the words of the prophets.[6] He then declares the decision:

> Therefore I have reached the decision that we should not trouble those Gentiles who are turning to God, but we should write to them to abstain only from things polluted by idols and from fornication and from whatever has been strangled and from blood. For in every city, for generations past, Moses has had those who proclaim

him, for he has been read aloud every sabbath in the
synagogues. (Acts 15:19–21)

But the decision does not conclude the process of discernment; it
must be put into action. "Then the apostles and the elders, with
the consent of the whole church, decided to choose men from
among their members and to send them to Antioch with Paul and
Barnabas" (v. 22). They are to bring a letter from the "apostles
and the elders, to the believers of Gentile origin in Antioch and
Syria and Cilicia." (v. 23), reiterating the decision made in
Jerusalem. Later, when the letter is read in Antioch, it is received
with enthusiasm there.

In examining the story of Peter's encounter with Cornelius,
four themes are raised around the discernment process: importance of prayer, role of openness, the relationship between tradition and present experience, and the place of narrative. Reviewing
the Council of Jerusalem through these themes deepens our understanding of them.

While explicit mention is not given to prayer, there are two
places in particular where a presumption of prayer would be
appropriate. In Acts 15:12, we are told that those gathered were in
silence as they heard the reports from Paul and Barnabas. In his
analysis of this story, theologian Avery Dulles points out that
silence and prayer are often linked in Luke's writing, and whether
the listeners in Acts 15 were in silent prayer or simply had no
refute for the Apostle's account, it is reasonable to presume that
prayer was a part of the discernment process.[7] Similarly, the
claim made later that they were speaking for the Holy Spirit presumes the presence of prayer: "For it has seemed good to the Holy
Spirit and to us to impose on you no further burden than these
essentials" (Acts 15:28).

In the discussion of Peter and Cornelius, we note the importance of openness to God's action and leadings that needs to permeate discernment. Openness and transparency is essential as we
discuss discernment within the community context. Throughout
Acts 15, we have accounts of Paul and Barnabas honestly speaking

their experience; whether greeted with joy and enthusiasm or suspicion and critique, they were open and transparent about what they regarded as the working of God in their lives and the lives of the Gentiles. This openness was the foundation for the Council in Jerusalem.

The conversation in Jerusalem is the quintessential example of the intersection between tradition and present experience, memory and future—the third theme traced in the examination of the account of Peter and Cornelius. As noted earlier, it is the conflict between two sets of values—the preservation of Jewish law and the full inclusion of Christians of Gentile origins—that makes this a matter for discernment. The decision reached at Jerusalem is one that honored both perspectives. Scripture scholar Timothy Luke Johnson makes an important point when noting that the basic dietary rules—abstaining from food sacrificed to idols or from meat of animals that has been strangled or from blood—were the one required set of rules. He points out that "this is the sort of regulation that comes into play precisely in the context of eating together, that is, fellowship. And it is intended to enable those who are sincere keepers of the Law to engage in such fellowship with the Gentiles."[8] Consequently, the application of this law is not for the sake of the law but for the sake of the community.

Finally, as in the story of Peter in Acts 10, the account of the Council of Jerusalem is rich with the narratives of people trying to live into a new situation. Each tells the tale of how he came to recognize in a new way the reality that Jesus' work of salvation is for everyone. It is in attending to these stories with care that the resolution of the dilemma is disclosed.

This brief tour through these two accounts of discernment—one for the individual and the other for the community—highlights the place of prayer and the importance of openness to God's action in the lives of individuals and communities; those involved were open to recognizing God's presence and sharing that with others. It is often within that narrative—the story of God's action in human lives—that both the simplicity and complexity of the issue under discernment is made clear. On the one hand, it is simple because it is about God's love for each person and God's hope for their freedom and salvation. On the other hand, it is complex because it takes place within the midst of human history and the challenge of balancing memory of the past with openness to the future. Living into that balance is an ongoing process.

DISCERNMENT IN CHRISTIAN LIFE TODAY

Clearly, discernment is a multilayered process that goes beyond simply weighing the pros and cons and making a decision. In many ways, it is more a way of life than an application of set steps around a specific issue. The discussion of discernment in Christian life today begins by defining or describing discernment in a way that is wide enough to include all its components and yet narrow enough to be meaningful. Then, consideration is given to three expressions of discernment: as way of life, as personal process, and as communal engagement.

Delineating Discernment

Each author who engages the topic of discernment finds him- or herself wandering around in an attempt to provide an adequate definition or at least description of the concept. At times, an author will provide a constrained description of discernment in one chapter only to broaden it in the next, or vice versa, providing a sweeping view of the concept in one section and then define it in a way that limits it to one aspect of the discernment process a few pages later. Earlier, we cited Lonsdale's description of discernment as a helpful guide to our discussion: as "allowing our deepest attitudes, aspirations, values, and relationships to come to the surface, so that it is they which give shape and direction to our choices."

In part, the challenge of defining discernment is that it rests at the intersection of a series of contrasting dimensions. Here we highlight four contrasting dimensions: First, discernment or the capacity to discern is both a gift and a habit that is enhanced with practice. In the first letter to the Corinthians, Paul speaks of the many gifts of the Spirit, one of which is the discernment of spirits (1 Cor 12:10). At the same time, our ability to discern is enhanced by our own commitment and practice.

Second, discernment is both a lifestyle perspective and a process for making a specific decision. In *The Discerning Heart*, Wilkie Au and Noreen Cannon Au propose that

> discernment is both a posture and a process. As a spiritual posture, discernment entails fostering a contemplative attitude that helps us to spot the presence of God in the concrete events and experiences of ordinary life.... As a process, discernment involves making decisions in a way that allows God to be a telling influence in our choices. The goal is to refine the acoustics of our heart so that we can better hear the Spirit's guidance.[9]

Openness to God's presence in our lives around a particular decision—an essential dimension of discernment—can only take place if we foster that openness throughout our lives. This is examined further in the next section.

Third, discernment is both an individual process and a communal one. As we saw in the two excerpts from Acts, Peter's discernment as an individual was both informed by and had a significant impact on the decisions of the community. Discernment is never just an individual or a communal activity; there is a dynamic interchange between these two aspects. Fourth, discernment is both a rational and an extra-rational practice. Not only do we need to think carefully through the pros and cons of a decision, gather information, and discuss perspective with others; we also need to be open to the movement of the spirit in our lives, listening to the inner response at each step of the way. Wilkie Au and Noreen Cannon Au write, "A purely rational approach to discernment is impoverished because it fails to recognize God's influence in religious and affective experiences."[10] Am I feeling comfortable with this decision; do I have a sense of affirmation about the next steps

I am taking? Or do I have a feeling of disquiet when I think about the decision, a sense that something just doesn't fit?[11] This affective dimension is an important part of the discernment process and one that needs to be nurtured for many of us.

Let us now examine these four dimensions of discernment further as we explore its three expressions: as way of life, as personal practice, and as communal process.

Discernment as Way of Life

In her book *The Writing Life*, Annie Dillard states, "How we spend our days is, of course, how we spend our lives."[12] This is very true around the experience of discernment: it is by fostering an awareness of God's presence and movement in our lives on a day-to-day basis that we enhance the capacity to apply the practice of discernment in the case of life's significant decisions. As we nurture this posture of discernment, we align our way of viewing the world more in keeping with God's desires and hopes for us. Elizabeth Liebert expresses the connection between discernment as way of life and as decision making in these terms: "Discernment is far more than the decisions we make. It is a discriminating way of life in which we come to notice with increasing ease and accuracy how our inner and outer actions affect our identity in God. Practicing discernment in decision making is but one aspect of this whole way of life."[13]

This view of discernment as way of life or posture is built upon a certain theological anthropology, that is, a way of understanding who God is, who human beings are, and how God and human beings are in relationship with one another. At its heart is the conviction that God is, in fact, present and communicating with us through our experience as human beings in the world. As our creator, God made us with a fundamental openness to God's presence; we are made to be in connection and relationship with God. And more than simply connected with God, we are made to be a participating agent in God's creative and redemptive action in the world. Through human experience—particularly experiences of great joy and wonder and beauty or experiences of loss and sin and the recognition of our own limitations[14]—we are able to be aware of God as the horizon of our being, the backdrop against which and the context within which we "live and move and have our being" (Acts 17:28).

But these experiences need to be interpreted. How do they become meaningful for us? They give us a sense of who God is and what God hopes for us through the application of the God-given gifts of reason, feelings, and imagination. Through human reason, we bring our experience into dialogue with the Christian tradition, recognizing the link between our experience and the experience of those in the past. Through human reason, we use the lens of the tradition to interpret and understand our experience. By identifying and listening to our feelings, we become aware of the present of God's presence; we develop the capacity to be in the present moment, which is where God is to be found. And through engaging the imagination, we envisage the future of God's presence; we imagine how we live into God's desires and hopes for us into our future.

While we are created with the capacity to know God and to recognize God's presence in our lives, we are not always aware of that presence. We do not always align our wills with God's desires and hopes for us. How does this aligning take place? Fundamentally, we approximate this by regularly engaging in those practices that enhance our awareness of God's presence and action in our lives and invite us to reflect on our participation in God's desires and hopes for us. The Christian tradition has a rich assortment of such practices; one of the most basic and effective is the daily examen.

Rooted in the spirituality and practice of Ignatius of Loyola, the examen is a practice that brings to our awareness the experiences of God's presence and call in our lives through the integration of reason, feelings, and imagination. While there are a variety of descriptions for how to do the examen, this prayer, which is generally done at the end of the day (or any block of time, such as week, semester, period of retreat, and so on) has four main elements. First, be aware of yourself as being in God's presence and ask for the light of the Spirit in your reflections. Second, review the day in terms of words, desires, actions, feelings, and so on. Then, express gratitude for the gifts of the day, and sorrow and purpose of amends for failings. Last, ask for the graces desired for the next day.[15] Regularly engaging in this process heightens awareness of God's presence not only at the time of prayer but throughout the day.

The intentional integration of practices that enhance our awareness of God's action in our lives become resources for living our lives in light of God's grace and making decisions reflective of God's hopes and intentions. It is to this second element of discernment—the process of decision making at both the individual and communal levels—that we now turn.

Making Decisions *for* Myself but Not *by* Myself

We all make decisions every day, all day: What route do I take to work? What will I have for lunch? Am I going to finish this project now, or put it off until tomorrow? Should I let the kids stay up late to watch a TV program or insist that they follow their usual bed time? Most of the time, they are made fairly easily, often without extensive conscious thought. That is not to say that these decisions are not of significance. For example, if I take the slightly shorter but more nerve-racking route, I arrive at work feeling on edge and stressed; is that the best way to go? What I eat for lunch has nutritional, economic, and ecological implications: what kind of world am I contributing to by my eating habits? However, in light of the discussion of discernment as way of life, these and even more complex day-to-day decisions are made more easily and with more of a sense of centeredness when we regularly engage in practices that enhance our awareness of God's presence in our lives. As we develop habits that help us align our own thinking and will with this awareness, our day-to-day decisions are more apt to be reflective of God's desires and hopes for us.

At other times, we are called to make more weighty decisions, those that call us to rethink how we invest our resources of time, energy, talent, and finances. These can include decisions with what appear to be short-term implications: Do I agree to serve as a catechist in our parish program this year? Do I become involved in the election campaign of a candidate I support? Do I make a commitment to contribute regularly and significantly to a charitable organization? Others have more long-term consequences: Shall I marry this person or not? Will we have children and is that to be by birth or adoption? Does my sense of dissatisfaction about my job mean a change in career or a shift in other priorities?

The practice of discernment invites us into a more intentional process as a way of addressing the complexity of the decision at hand; it is a process that can be helpful to share with individuals and communities of practice so that there is a common understanding of discernment as it is used within a parish or pastoral setting. While there is a variety of ways to describe the process, these elements are common to most of them.[16]

Move toward an Inner Disposition of Freedom

Entering the process of discernment with our heart and hopes already invested in a particular outcome is not a recipe for effective discernment. Suspending our preconceived notions of what "ought" to be the results of our discernment and being genuinely open to the movement of the Spirit in our discernment is essential. The process of decision making within this context proceeds from a sense of freedom: interior freedom that allows us to be open to new possibilities. Ignatius of Loyola spoke of this as "holy indifference." We are indifferent to the outcomes of our discernment. This does not mean we don't care; we care deeply, but not about the specific decision we reach. We care that our decision is one that is in keeping with and in service to God's desires and hopes for us and for the world.

Name and Clarify the Issue at Hand

At times, we can feel so confused that the only question we can ask is "What am I going to do with my life?" This all-encompassing question is a difficult starting place for the discernment process. Deciding to take a job opportunity that is basically in one's present field of work and the broader question of considering a vocational change are two different expressions of discernment. Through prayer, reflection, journaling, or talking with a friend or spiritual director, we come to name more clearly the fundamental concern, or the concern about which we can take action. The very process of articulating for ourselves the core decision to be discerned is itself part of the process by which we come to greater clarity about the parameters of our decision.

Gather Data

Many decisions require us to do the legwork of gathering information and talking with lots of people. This involves asking ourselves, "What do I need to know in order to make this decision?" Sometimes, this requires research into a specific option that we are weighing: "Do I take this job or not?" Other times, it is about looking into several options and possibilities: "How do I sort through the option of where to invest my time and energy in service to others?" In any case, doing the research is an important part of discernment and should not be short-changed.

Pray, Reflect, and Imagine

While listed as one item of many, this element of the discernment process really runs throughout each of the steps. The attitude of prayer and awareness of God's presence, which are the foundation of a discerning way of life, are at the heart of this process as well. Continually reminding ourselves that we are in the presence of a God who cares for us and desires good for us frames our openness to the data we collect and the options that arise. Here also, the gifts of human reason, feelings, and imagination come into play. It is through applying our human reason that we are able to analyze and evaluate the information gathered and think through possible options. Naming and engaging the affective dimension provide further insight and information to the process.

Our own feelings of excitement, concern, trepidation, challenge, and so forth need to be examined for their source and implications as they guide us in the process of discernment. Finally, our imagination is a valuable resource. Imagining ourselves living out some of the options that our research, reason, and feelings point to helps them feel more "real" to us; more as genuine options with positive and negative consequences. These experiences also provide us with further data for prayer and reflection.

Formulate a Tentative Decision

In light of reflection, prayer, and imagination, we come to a tentative decision: to proceed with a job or not, to look into some aspect of service in the community rather than others. It is a *tentative* decision because we still need to complete the final element.

Seek Confirmation

While talking with friends, family, and spiritual guides is important in the overall process of discernment, in seeking confirmation of a tentative decision, our clearest source is our own response. In his book that focuses specifically on Ignatian patterns of discernment, Mark Thibodeaux writes about the role of reflecting on one's inner response to a decision as essential to the processes of confirmation:

> Ignatius boldly trusts a praying person's deep desires. So, as I move deeper into one choice and away from others, are my deep desires consistently in favor of this change? (Remember that we are talking here about *deep* desires. Even if the option *is* God's will, there will always be more superficial attractions to the other options.) Do I sense joyful anticipation or at least tranquil acceptance as I consider living with the consequences of this decision? Or, is there instead a deep sense of dread?[17]

When we are people of prayer, committed to seeking decisions reflective of God's hopes for us, being attentive to our deep desires is the most reliable source of confirmation for us. Once confirmed by our own sense of consolation, we can proceed with our decision, confident that we have opened ourselves up to God's presence in our lives and are living in response to that.

Three caveats to this description of the discernment process are to be noted: First, while listed here in a linear way, the various elements of discernment often weave in and out among each other in reality. The process of clarifying the question involves research; prayer, reflection, and imagination permeate all of the elements. Second, everyone's experience is different. Some people find that their major decisions seem to arrive fully developed in their thinking and imagining. Others expend a good deal of time and energy naming the issue, exploring the options, and so on. When rooted in a practice of regular prayer and followed with the intention of shaping our lives in light of God's hopes for us, we can say that it is good discernment. Third, can a discernment process "go wrong"? After a process of discernment, I take a new job; three months later, the company is bought out and I am laid off. Is that a "bad" discernment? That may be the wrong question. It is the intention and commitment to direct our will and decisions in light of God's desires and hopes as we come to know them that makes for a "good" discernment process.

From Votes toward Accord

Thinking about the way in which discernment is integrated into the life of a community raises the same two concerns discussed in reference to individual discernment: How do we establish a context where discernment is possible and supported, and what elements make up the process of discernment within a community?

In many ways, the elements that are at the heart of the process for individual discernment are also present in communal discernment, with the added dimension of this being a shared activity among the members. Consequently, for communal discernment, the process includes a clear articulation and shared understanding of the question at hand; gathering, sharing, and analyzing appropriate data; prayer, reflection, and imagining, both as individuals and as a community; proposing and agreeing upon tentative decisions; and seeking confirmation by attending to the inner response of the participants to the decision and by identifying the ways in which the decision resonates with the community's identity and shared endeavor. While this process can be challenging as a group, the more daunting task is nurturing an environment where such a process can happen. In reflecting on models of discernment, Frank Rogers writes, "Both Ignatian and Quaker forms of communal discernment require a great deal from participants, who must intentionally try both to seek their own wisdom about God's direction for the community and to open themselves to the wisdom of the other participants."[18]

For discernment within a community of practice, an important beginning point is a shared understanding that the goal of discernment is more than simply reaching the most sensible or prudent decision. Rooted in the work of communal discernment is a shared commitment to a process by which the group can come to a decision that is reflective of God's hopes for the community and its members. As with individual discernment, this process begins by fostering an awareness of the work of the Spirit within the community of practice. A sometimes perfunctory opening prayer or a vague recognition of the Spirit's presence will generally not suffice in awakening this awareness. Integrating prayer into the life of the CoP and having that prayer connect with the wider community sets a firmer foundation for developing a spirit of discernment within the group.

For the characteristics of a community open to discernment, we can return to the elements we examined in the prior three chapters: hospitality, conversation, and followership. Taken together, these three ways of being in community encompass the primary descriptors of a discerning community: a capacity to listen, a spirit of openness and trust, a willingness to articulate a position while acknowledging its limitations, communication with a wider constituency, and freedom to allow the Spirit to guide the group in directions not yet traveled.[19]

IMPLICATIONS FOR COMMUNITIES OF PRACTICE

As we examine the implications of discernment for communities of practice, it is helpful to consider it both in terms of the individuals in the CoPs as well as the community itself as an agent of discernment. In both cases, we need to consider both the context within which discernment is supported and the process by which that happens.

Inviting People into Discernment

A foundational element of fostering a spirit of discernment within the CoPs and among their members could involve having a process set up within the parish where individuals can be made aware of a process of discernment and its potential as a guiding force in their lives. If people's decisions to join a particular CoP is guided by a process of Christian discernment, that dynamic will get carried over to the work of the CoP itself. If carefully planned and assiduously followed up on, an annual parish-wide "Time, Talents, and Treasures" survey that lists the various areas in which parishioners can be involved can be an effective way of garnering volunteers for the various established activities and programs. But this is often quite separate from any models or process of discernment. It simply states the needs of the parish. Here, we are looking from the other direction—not so much what the parish needs but what the person is being called to do.

Imagine inviting, once or twice a year, newly registered members of the parish community to gather with other established parishioners for a simple meal and a structured conversation on the topic of discernment. How did they make significant decisions in their lives? What decisions led to their registering in this parish?

What aspects of their lives are most in the midst of flux? The point, here, is not to have them volunteer for parish activities, but to recognize the way God is or might be part of their decision-making processes. The gathering closes with a simple examen and an invitation to participate in one or two further gatherings of smaller groups to explore the process of discernment and the role it can play in their lives. These subsequent meetings provide guidance on how to foster a spirit of discernment as well as an actual process one might use in making a decision.

Again, the primary purpose is not to recruit more volunteers; it would be providing a context where a discerning lifestyle and a model of discernment can be taught and fostered.

Giving People Options

A second way of enhancing the role of discernment in the life of the individual member of a CoP is to be intentional about inviting people into a particular community of practice *and* inviting them out. In chapter 3, we examined the idea that new members are essential for the life and vitality of the community of practice. They bring both continuity, as they learn from experienced members and further the shared endeavor of the group, and discontinuity, as they introduce new ideas, raise questions, and contribute to the ongoing shaping of the CoP's work. In most cases, however, for new members to come in, experienced members need to move out.

In some contexts—the pastoral council, for example—there are established periods of membership/service; in most parish roles—catechist, lector, and member of a committee or advisory board—that is not the case. One way to address this is to ask for a specific time commitment when inviting people into a particular ministry. At the end of the agreed upon time—two years, three years, whatever seems appropriate for the level of work and commitment—thank them for their service. Renewing their commitment, if appropriate, is a different step, which can be addressed separately.

For commitments that have a logical beginning and end—members of an RCIA team and catechists, for example, sending a note of thanks at the end of the year and then a separate invitation to join again as plans for the following year get underway provides the opportunity for people to opt in or out. Setting the invitation to join/re-join in the context of prayer and discernment encourages participants to recognize the place of discernment in their engagement with the CoPs of the parish.

Creating Space for a Spirit of Discernment

Throughout this book, reference has been made to the importance of integrating a spirit of prayer into the rhythm of communities of practice. The CoPs have been presented here as an essential way in which the faith of many adults within the parish community is enhanced and deepened. Furthermore, it is in the context of creating a space for discernment that the presence of a spirit of prayer comes to fruition; discernment is rooted in a way of being—both as individuals and as communities—that is marked by an awareness of God's presence strengthened by prayer.

Other communal practices that contribute to a spirit of discernment include open conversation, reflection, silence, and an opportunity to discuss experiences of awareness of God's presence. In other words, for groups and committees that focus on a narrow view of accomplishing tasks rather than the broader shared endeavor that includes the faith formation of its members, the move toward a more discernment-oriented approach to decision making could be challenging.[20] As noted already, attention to the elements of conversation, hospitality, and followership helps to shape a community that is open to the work of discernment.

Establishing a CoP's Process of Discernment

The final implication of discernment for communities of practice is that the community be intentional about establishing a process of communal discernment that is readily and regularly employed as the need arises. Knowing that certain procedural guidelines are used when making significant decisions is helpful to the cohesion of the group and its discerning spirit. Such guidelines might include the following: final decisions on a topic should not be made at the same meeting at which the topic was introduced; time for silence and reflection should be integrated into the decision process; each person has the opportunity to express his or her opinion or position as part of the decision process; care should be taken to be particularly attentive to those holding a minority opinion; significant decisions should be reviewed again at a meeting following their tentative acceptance in order to seek confirmation.

While not every decision requires the same time and attention, each decision and all deliberations are best made in a spirit of prayer and openness to the guidance of the Spirit in the lives of the members and the community itself.

CONVERSATION AND REFLECTION

1. Recall your opening reflection: *Think about a significant decision you have made. What process was involved in coming to the decision? What roles did other people, reasoning with pro and con lists, gathering information, or prayer play in the decision making? Did you think of that as discernment? Why or why not?*

   In what ways has this chapter confirmed, enhanced, and/or challenged your understanding of discernment? Do the ideas from this chapter shed new light on your understanding of the process of decision making?

2. The distinction was made within our understanding of discernment between way of life and approach to decision making, between posture and process. How is this distinction helpful? How do these two elements come together in your own life?

3. How is the dimension of discernment as way of life reflected in your communities of practice? What steps might you take to highlight, enhance, or strengthen that dimension?

4. As you reflect on the process of decision making within the communities of practice within your pastoral setting, are the observations for communal decision making outlined above helpful? Why or why not? How might you be more intentional about incorporating some of those elements into your CoPs?

We have seen that discernment is not a technique for making decisions or a new approach to help working groups reach consensus. It is a perspective and a process that is rooted in a confidence of God's presence in the world and a willingness to be open to the Spirit's guidance as we seek to live into and out of God's hopes and desires for us.

Chapter 8

LEANING IN THE RIGHT DIRECTION

As we look to the process of establishing communities of practice within a pastoral context, the following story, which has been shared in a number of settings, is appropriate. Early in my work as a parish catechetical leader, I was convinced of the need to change the focus of faith formation from children to adults. But I was overwhelmed by the challenges of bringing such a vision into reality. My pastor, encouraging of my work and supportive of its direction, heard my frustration and gave me great guidance: "Remember, if you can't move in the right direction, at least lean that way!"

The direction this book is encouraging you to lean is toward integrating the concept of communities of practice into your pastoral setting in order to facilitate the faith formation of the members and, through them, the parish's capacity to become a more effective agent of evangelization. This final point is important. We imagine our parish committees and gatherings in terms of communities of practice not because that makes them more effective and efficient—though I believe it does do that in the long run—but because of our fundamental task: the work of evangelization.

Viewing the parish through the lens of communities of practice is being intentional about recognizing and articulating our shared enterprise, about doing the work of the CoP through a process of mutual engagement, and about being attentive to the community's shared repertoire. Of particular importance in our context is recognizing the shared enterprise in terms of three concentric circles: the task of a particular gathering that is situated within the overall charge of the group, which is itself set in (and really makes the most sense within) the general thrust of the parish, to be about the mission of the church.

In addition to being about the way a community interacts within itself and with others and thus accomplishes its goals, the early chapters of this book also presented the idea that it is through participation in CoPs that the identity of the members are formed. The participants come to see themselves through the lens of the knowledge they have gained and the practices in which they have engaged. For this conversation, an essential consideration became how these CoPs can also enhance the faith of the members. In addition to integrating specific practices into each CoP—time for prayer and reflection, for example, or connecting it with the larger community of faith—there are also key dimensions that need to be considered as part of each CoP and of the parish as a constellation of CoPs: hospitality, conversation, followership, and discernment.

In these closing pages is an invitation to integrate the concept of communities of practice into your pastoral setting through suggestions as to how you might "lean that way."

REMEMBER THE BROAD-BASED ENDEAVOR

If you are the DRE in a parish or a campus minister in a school or hold other such positions and find yourself thinking about how you might integrate these ideas into the wider pastoral setting, it is essential that you step back and recognize that this is not your job...or, at least, not your job alone. Within the parish, any talk of faith formation can easily fall on the shoulders of the catechetical leader(s), and while he or she may be a key instigator, the vision that is being proposed here goes beyond one element of the life of the parish. A good way to begin might be to have others read this book and then engage in conversation around its applicability in your pastoral setting.

RECOGNIZE WHAT YOU ARE ALREADY DOING

You may already be integrating some or many of the ideas and suggestions that I have given in the book. Many of them, around the themes of conversation and hospitality, for example, are not unique to communities of practice. But the discussion of communities of practice may provide a framework for how the various practices in which you already engage make sense together. As you begin to lean in the direction of creating communities of practice, recognize and affirm the ways in which they already exist in an, as yet, unnamed way.

BEGIN WITH THOSE COMMITTEES AND GROUPS OF WHICH YOU ARE A MEMBER OR LEADER

If you are the youth minister, you will probably have a hard time forming the ushers or the choir into a community of practice. Begin where your own role intersects with the life of the parish; begin with committees and boards of which you are a member. If you are the DRE, what steps would you take to shape your catechists, or a subgroup of your catechists in a large parish, into a community of practice that is not only about accomplishing its task but enhancing the faith life of the catechists themselves, keeping in mind the larger picture of evangelization? That is where you might best begin as you lean into this vision.

BE EXPLICIT ABOUT WHAT YOU ARE TRYING TO ACHIEVE

Change is seldom easy or in many cases welcomed, as people believe they already do their roles effectively and efficiently. To introduce and implement the essential elements of communities of practice will require some changes. Adults react more positively when they have a sense of where they are going and why the changes are being made. Taking the time to present your understanding of communities of practice and the potential for integrating it into the life of the parish, or at least into the working of a particular group, will serve as a good foundation for later changes you introduce.

PRAY FOR YOUR PARISH OR PASTORAL SETTING

Most importantly, make it your practice to pray for your parish and the communities of practice that constitute it. Our work is challenging and our task demanding: to be and become effective agents of evangelizations, "bringing the Good News into all the strata of humanity, and through its influence transforming humanity from within and making it new" (*Evangelii Nuntiandi* 18). That can only be done through the grace of God and the work of the Spirit. Be confident of those gifts present in your parish today.

NOTES

CHAPTER 1

1. During the years that I taught introductory undergraduate courses both at St. John's University in Collegeville, Minnesota, and at Boston College, the first assignment was to write a three-to-four–page essay describing the elements or experiences that have had a significant influence—positive or negative—on your understanding of God or church or faith. One striking point was that the negative influences were varied and reflected a number of themes. The positive experiences could almost all be grouped under one of three headings: a specific person who listened during a challenging time, a service experience, or a retreat experience.

2. At three places in Acts, there are summary descriptions (somewhat idealized, perhaps) of the early Christian community: Acts 2:42–47; 4:32–37; 5:12–16.

3. In "Our Hearts Were Burning Within Us," the 1999 document on adult faith formation from the United States Catholic Conference of Bishops, these three dimensions are named as the fundamental goals of adult faith formation; see nos. 68–73 (Washington, DC: USCCB Publishing, 1999).

4. *Ad Gentes* (AG), "On the Missionary Activity of the Church" (1965), http://www.vatican.va/archive/hist_councils/ii_vatican_council/documents/vat-ii_decree_19651207_ad-gentes_en.html.

5. Pope Paul VI, *Evangelii Nuntiandi* (EN), "Apostolic Exhortation on Evangelization" (1975), http://www.vatican.va/holy_father/paul_vi/apost_exhortations/documents/hf_p-vi_exh_19751208_evangelii-nuntiandi_en.html.

6. Pope John Paul II, *Catechesi Tradendae* (CT), "Apostolic Exhortation on Catechesis" (1979), http://www.vatican.va/holy_father/

john_paul_ii/apost_exhortations/documents/hf_jp-ii_exh_16101979_
catechesi-tradendae_en.html.

7. Pope John Paul II, *Christifideles Laici* (CL), "Apostolic Exhortation on the Laity" (1988), http://www.vatican.va/holy_father/ john_paul_ii/apost_exhortations/documents/hf_jp-ii_exh_30121988_ christifideles-laici_en.html.

8. Pope John Paul II, *Redemptoris Missio* (RM), "On the Church's Mission Activity" (1990), http://www.vatican.va/holy_father/john_paul_ ii/encyclicals/documents/hf_jp-ii_enc_07121990_redemptoris-missio_ en.html.

9. Congregation for the Clergy, *General Directory for Catechesis* (Washington, DC: USCCB, 1998), http://www.vatican.va/roman_curia/ congregations/cclergy/documents/rc_con_ccatheduc_doc_17041998_ directory-for-catechesis_en.html.

10. For background on the genre of directory and an analysis of this document, see Jane E. Regan and Michael P. Horan, *Good News in New Forms* (Washington, DC: National Conference of Catechetical Leaders, 2000).

11. For further analysis of the Pope John Paul II understanding of new evangelization, see Avery Dulles, "John Paul II and the New Evangelization," *America* 166, no. 3 (1992): 52–59, 69–72; and Peter John McGregor, "New World, New Pentecost, New Church," *Compass* 12, no. 5 (2012): 18–31.

CHAPTER 2

1. All citations to this document are given by paragraph number in the text.

2. Cf. the work of Etienne Wenger and Jean Lave, whose works are directed toward business. See Jean Lave and Etienne Wenger, *Situated Learning: Legitimate Peripheral Participation* (New York: Cambridge University Press, 1991); Etienne Wenger, *Communities of Practice: Learning, Meaning and Identity* (Cambridge University Press, 1998); Etienne Wenger, Richard A. McDermott, and William Snyder, *Cultivating Communities of Practice: A Guide to Managing Knowledge* (Boston, MA: Harvard Business School Press, 2002). More recently, their constructs have been adapted in educational settings, see, for example, *Communities*

of Practice: Creating Learning Environments for Educators, ed. Chris Kimble, Paul Hildreth (Charlotte, NC: Information Age, 2008).

3. There are a variety of ways in which "practice" is used in contemporary religious education. See, for example, the work of Dorothy C. Bass, who directs the Valparaiso Project on the Education and Formation of People in Faith as well as the writing of Craig Dykstra. Bass and Dykstra describe Christian practices as "things Christian people do together over time to address fundamental human needs in response to and in the light of God's active presence for the life of the world." See "A Theological Understanding of Christian Practices," *Lifelong Faith* (Summer 2008): 6. As we talk about "communities of practice" within the Christian context, I am emphasizing the social aspect of practice and its role in shaping identity. Cf. Alasdair MacIntyre, *After Virtue*, 3rd ed. (Notre Dame: University of Notre Dame Press, 2007), 187ff.

4. Cf. Wenger, *Communities of Practice*. These terms take on a technical meaning and are used that way throughout this book.

5. In *Community of Practice*, Wenger writes, "Being included in what matters is a requirement for being engaged in a community's practice" (74). In this context, what matters is the members' participation and contribution to the shape that the shared endeavor of a particular community takes.

6. In Wenger's work, for example, he speaks of modes of belonging that he names *engagement, imagination,* and *alignment.* See *Community of Practice*, 173–87. He develops this further in "Communities of Practice and Social Learning Systems," *Organization* 7, no. 2 (2000): 225–46. I develop this idea in a somewhat different direction by emphasizing the core interests and scope of those whose dominant mode of engagement is marked by either internal concerns or external relationships.

7. For a more detailed list of possible indicators, see Wenger, *Community of Practice*, 125–26.

8. For a discussion of the importance of narrative—telling "war stories"—to the effectiveness of communities of practice, see John Seely Brown, Allan Collins, and Paul Duguid, "Situated Cognition and the Culture of Learning," in *Situated Learning Perspectives*, ed. Hilary McLellan (Englewood Cliffs, NJ: Educational Technology Publications, 1996), 40.

9. See Lave and Wenger, *Situated Learning*, particularly chap. 1.

10. Ibid., 29.

11. Hansman, "Adult Learning in Communities of Practice," 298.

12. Brown, Collins, and Duguid describe authentic activities as "the ordinary practices of the culture" in counterpoint to school activities, which are, at best, hybrids: circumscribed by one culture (school) while giving attribution to another culture (e.g., readers, writers, believers). "Situated Cognition and the Culture of Learning," 25.

13. In *Situated Learning*, Lave and Wenger examine the dynamics of apprenticeship by looking at midwives, tailors, quartermasters, butchers, and nondrinking alcoholics.

14. See Lave and Wenger, *Situated Learning*, 69–72.

15. The apprentice does not rely simply on the master but comes to learn that it is in the situation of the apprenticeship that the mastery lies. Lave and Wenger write, "To take a decentered view of master-apprentice relations leads to an understanding that mastery resides not in the master but in the organization of the community of practice of which the master is part." *Situated Learning*, 94.

16. Lave and Wenger make the point that learning within the context of apprenticeship moves beyond the limiting teacher-learner or even master-apprentice relationship. Learning as legitimate peripheral participation means having interaction with old-timers, peers, and newcomers. "The diversified field of relations among old-timers and newcomers within and across the various cycles, and the importance of near-peers in the circulation of knowledgeable skills, both recommend against assimilating relations of learning to the dyadic form characteristic of conventional learning studies." *Situated Learning*, 57.

17. Lave and Wenger write, "Legitimate peripheral participation refers both to the development of knowledgeably skilled identities in practice and to the reproduction and transformation of communities of practice. It concerns the latter insofar as communities of practice consist of and depend on membership, including its characteristic biographies/trajectories, relationships, and practices." *Situated Learning*, 55.

18. Wenger speaks of membership in communities of practice being both about power and about vulnerability: "On the one hand, it is the power to belong, to be a certain person, to claim a place with the legitimacy of membership; and on the other it is the vulnerability of belonging to, of identifying with, and being part of some communities that contribute to defining who we are and thus have a hold on us." *Community of Practice*, 207.

19. It is important to note that simply being lectors in the same parish does not constitute a community of practice. In many parishes, the lectors have little mutual engagement; they come in for the assigned liturgy and may have little or no contact with other lectors. The lector group that meets on Saturday morning is a community of practice in that it has a shared enterprise, mutual engagement, and common repertoire.

20. Wenger makes the point that there are two expressions of non-participation: peripherality, when the member selects to remain at the periphery him or herself, and the other is marginality, when the dynamics of the group press the member toward the boundaries. *Community of Practice*, 165–69.

CHAPTER 3

1. See Wenger, *Communities of Practice*, 127.

2. Ibid.

3. See chapter 5 for a more extended discussion of the importance of conversation to the growth of faith and the life of CoPs.

4. We refer here primarily to identifiable, explicit communities of practice—the practitioners of catechesis within St. Odo the Good parish, the practitioners of proclamation of the Word, and so on; there is also a sense in which we can talk about CoPs being more broadly understood as parents of young children, high school teachers, newscasters. Although these might be seen as global categories, the reality is that we experience these communities at the local level. Being the parent of adult children at this time and in this place shapes my identity. See Wenger, *Communities of Practice*, 131–33 for a discussion of the relationship between local and global.

5. "Renewing members" refers to two different groups. The first are often referred to as "returning Catholics"—those who, for a variety of reasons, have been absent from the faith community. The second are those who have maintained a basic relationship with the parish—perhaps simply attending Sunday liturgy fairly regularly—but have no real connection with the parish. Their membership in the parish has played a small role in shaping their identity and way of making meaning, and they wish to give it further attention.

6. See the discussion in chapter 2 concerning the role of more advanced apprentices in showing the newer ones the way.

7. See chapter 7 for a discussion of the role and means of discernment within the context of a CoP.

8. Wenger, *Communities of Practice*, 105.

9. See Etienne Wenger, "Communities of Practice and Social Learning Systems," *Organization* 7, no. 2 (May 2000): 236 for a discussion of these three elements—artifacts, language, and processes—as "boundary objects" that can serve as bridges between CoPs.

10. See Etienne Wenger, Richard McDermott, and William Snyder, *Cultivating Communities of Practice* (Boston: Harvard Business School Press, 2002), particularly 151–54.

11. Wenger, "Communities of Practice and Social Learning Systems," 233.

CHAPTER 4

1. Henri Nouwen, *Reaching Out: The Three Movements of the Spiritual Life* (New York: Image, 1986), 66.

2. Andrew Arterbury points to the haste and extravagance of Abraham's actions in *Entertaining Angels: Early Christian Hospitality in its Mediterranean Setting*, New Testament Monograph 8 (Scheffield: Scheffield Phoenix Press), 60.

3. John Koenig, *New Testament Hospitality: Partnership with Strangers as Promise and Mission* (Philadelphia: Fortress Press, 1985), 6.

4. See *Making Room: Recovering Hospitality as a Christian Tradition* (Grand Rapids, MI: Eerdmans, 1999), 27–29. See also, Letty M. Russell, *Just Hospitality: God's Welcome in a World of Difference* (Louisville, KY: John Knox, 2009), 83.

5. See Luke Bretherton, *Hospitality as Holiness: Christian Witness amid Moral Diversity* (Burlington, VT: Ashgate Publishing, 2006), 133, for a discussion of the implication of the hosts response in welcoming in strangers rather than seeking vengeance toward those who rejected him.

6. Joseph A. Fitzmyer, *The Gospel According to Luke X-XXIV*, The Anchor Yale Bible Commentaries (Garden City, NY: Doubleday, 1985), 1049–50.

7. Pohl, *Making Room*, 31.

8. Pope Francis, *Evangelii Gaudium* (EG), "The Joy of the Gospel" (2013), http://www.vatican.va/holy_father/francesco/apost_exhortations/documents/papa-francesco_esortazione-ap_20131124_evangelii-gaudium_en.html.

9. Pohl, *Making Room*, 172.

10. Parker J. Palmer, *The Company of Strangers: Christians and the Renewal of America's Public Life* (New York: Crossroad, 1983), 65.

11. Nouwen, *Reaching Out*, 87.

12. Russell, *Just Hospitality*, 2.

13. One approach to this question can be found in the analysis of human knowing and meaning making reflected in the perspective of constructive developmentalists. Here I am thinking particularly of the writing of Robert Kegan in his book *In over Our Heads: The Mental Demands of Modern Life* (Cambridge, MA: Harvard University Press, 1994). Here, he examines the way in which people grow in their ability to see their own positions and beliefs as valid but constructed ways of seeing the world. As such, they are always partial and open to critique. From this framework, the positions and beliefs of others provide a way for us to understand our own position more clearly. Kegan argues for the importance of being open to the positions of others without necessarily losing track of our own commitments.

CHAPTER 5

1. William Isaacs, *Dialogue and the Art of Thinking Together* (New York: Currency, 1999), 165.

2. Deborah Tanner, *The Argument Culture: Moving from Debate to Dialogue* (New York: Random House, 1998), 5.

3. For a fuller discussion of this image of God as one who initiates conversation, see Christoph Schwöbel, "God as Conversation: Reflection on a Theological Ontology of Communicative Relations," in *Theology and Conversation: Towards a Relational Theology*, ed. P. DeMay and J. Haers (Leuven: Leuven University Press, 2003), 43–68.

4. This story is recounted in each of the Synoptic Gospels with some variation. See Matthew 19:16–30 and Luke 18:18–30. Each version designates the man differently—the rich young man, the rich young ruler, or simply the man in Mark's version.

5. A question that arises from this story is what Jesus meant by the term "living water"? Exegetes propose that in using the term, Jesus is referring either to his own revelation and teaching or to the Spirit that he communicated to his followers. It is arguable that, based on John's use of symbols, both understandings are intended. See Raymond Brown, *The Gospel According to John I-XII*, Anchor Bible Series, vol. 29 (Garden City, NY: Doubleday, 1966), 178–79.

6. The woman's misinterpretation of the term "living water" can be seen as an example of the Gadamerian notion that misunderstanding precedes understanding. Hans Georg Gadamer, whose work on conversation comes up later in this chapter, argues that our "fore-meanings and prejudices" point us in an interpretive direction that may or may not be the meaning of the speaker. It is only through further conversation and openness to the alterity of the conversation partner that this can be resolved in favor of an accurate understanding. See Hans Georg Gadamer, *Truth and Method*, 2nd ed. (New York: Continuum, 1999), 268–69.

7. The reference here is to Mount Gerizim; see Deuteronomy 11:27.

8. "The Second Vatican Council marked a turning point in the development of a dialogical approach to the Catholic Church. Bishops and theologians who participated in the council laid the theological groundwork and identified the reform of key practices necessary for building a dialogical church." Bradford E. Hinze, *Practices of Dialogue in the Roman Catholic Church: Aims and Obstacles, Lessons and Laments* (New York: Continuum, 2006), 2.

9. Hinze, *Practices of Dialogue in the Roman Catholic Church*, 2. Note that Hinze uses "dialogue" and "conversation" synonymously in his book and, drawing on the work of Hans Georg Gadamer and David Tracy, describes dialogue as the back and forth communication between two or more (Hinze, *Practices of Dialogue in the Roman Catholic Church*, 10).

10. Hinze, *Practices of Dialogue in the Roman Catholic Church*, 6–8.

11. To take the Common Ground Initiative as an example, the range of critics included a number of cardinals; see Bernard Law, "Response to 'Called to be Catholic,'" *Origins* 21 (August 29, 1996): 170–71; and Avery Dulles, "The Travails of Dialogue," in *Church and Society:*

The Laurence J. McGinley Lectures, 1988-2007 (New York: Fordham University Press, 2008).

12. Popularized by educator and activist Paulo Freire, "conscientization" refers to the educational process by which the participants are made more aware of and question the presumptions underlying sociopolitical realities. Particular attention is given to the experience of oppression and the presumptions of those in power that support and further the status quo. Put simply, it is the way of building up one's awareness of social reality through reflection and action.

13. Thomas Groome, *Sharing Faith* (San Francisco: Harper, 1991), 156.

14. Gadamer, *Truth and Method*, 383.

15. This corresponds to the inquiry that is involved in the second movement of Shared Christian Praxis as described by Thomas Groom in *Sharing Faith*. Groome speaks about three dimensions of critical reflection: critical reasoning, critical remembering, and critical imagining, which can be expressed in the questions, Why do I act in the world around the given topic in the way that I do? What in my past contributed to my present action around this topic? and What future is being created by this way of being? See chapter 7 of *Sharing Faith*.

16. Isaacs, *Dialogue and the Art of Thinking Together*. See particularly "Part II: Building Capacities for New Behavior."

17. Ibid., 84.

18. Ibid., 111.

19. Ibid., 151.

20. Ibid., 159.

21. See chapter 2 for a discussion of the interrelationship of the three levels of tasks that each CoP addresses—the specific focus of the meeting, the broader task of the group in light of the parish, and the overarching goal in terms of the mission of the church.

CHAPTER 6

1. It is interesting to note that one of the first times the concept of "followership" appeared in an article title in a significant leadership journal was in 2006: David Collinson, "Rethinking Followership: A Poststructuralist Analysis of Follower Identities," *Leadership Quarterly* 17

(2006): 179–89. The term appeared for the first time in *Harvard Business Review* in 2001.

2. Francis J. Moloney and Daniel J. Harrington, *Gospel of John*, Sacra Pagina, 4 (Collegeville, MN: Liturgical Press, 1998), 54.

3. In a video covering this section of the Gospel of John, Daniel Harrington summarized it by saying, "So these are eight points or ways by which we find in the farewell discourse and the Last Supper discourse ways by which we can carry on the mission of Jesus: accepting salvation on its own terms, love, faith, the Holy Spirit, vital relationship with Jesus, people of hope, mission, and unity." Daniel Harrington and Thomas Stegman, "John's Gospel: Holy Week and Easter Themes," Encore video, posted by School of Theology and Ministry, Boston College, March 23, 2012, http://www.bc.edu/schools/stm/edevnts/CampusEvents/PastLectures/2012/3-23-12_4.html.

4. Documents of Vatican Council II, *Lumen Gentium* (LG), "The Dogmatic Constitution on the Church" (1964), http://www.vatican.va/archive/hist_councils/ii_vatican_council/documents/vat-ii_const_19641121_lumen-gentium_en.html.

5. Brian Gleeson, "Commemorating *Lumen Gentium*: A Short History of a Ground-breaking Charter," *Australian eJournal of Theology* 3 (August 2004), 2, http://aejt.com.au/__data/assets/pdf_file/0006/395655/AEJT_3.12_Gleeson.pdf. For a recent exposition on the document and its contribution to the understanding of church reflected here, see Richard R. Gaillardetz, *The Church in the Making:* Lumen gentium, Christus dominus, Orientalium ecclesiarum (New York: Paulist Press, 2006).

6. USCCB, *Called and Gifted for the Third Millennium* (Washington, DC: United States Catholic Conference, 1995).

7. One of the first to point to the importance of followers was management theorist Mary Parker Follett, who, in her 1949 book, *The Essentials of Leadership*, wrote that more research was needed into a topic "of utmost importance, but which has been far too little considered, and that's the part of followers." Quoted in Kent Bjugstad et al., "A Fresh Look at Followership: A Model for Matching Followership and Leadership Styles," *Journal of Behavioral and Applied Management* 7, no. 3 (April 2006): 304.

8. Systems thinking refers to the method of examining and analyzing organizations in terms of the interrelated components that mutually influence one another. Central to the significance of systems thinking is

"dynamic complexity," whereby cause and effect relationships are not always evident or where short-term impacts are different from long-term effects. The rise of interest in systems thinking within business and other organizations can be traced to the work of Peter Senge's book *The Fifth Discipline* (New York: Currency/Doubleday, 1990) in which he proposes systems thinking as the "fifth discipline" that serves to integrate the work of learning organizations, that is organizations that support the ongoing learning of all of its members and of all of its component parts. For a discussion of the application of the concept of learning organizations to schools, see John O'Neil, "On Schools as Learning Organizations: A Conversation with Peter Senge," http://patriciathinks.yolasite.com/resources/Senge.pdf. For a discussion of the application of learning organizations and systems thinking to parish life, see Jane E. Regan, "The Aim of Catechesis: Educating for an Adult Church," in *Horizons and Hopes: The Future of Religious Education*, ed. Thomas Groome and Harold Horell (New York: Paulist Press, 2003), see particularly 37–48.

9. Robert E. Kelley, "In Praise of Followers," *Harvard Business Review* 66 (November/December 1988): 142–48. Since then, and significantly increasing since the early 2000s, a number of books and articles examining followership have appeared. Many of the early ones tended to be theoretical and/or anecdotal; more recently, articles based in qualitative research have begun to appear.

10. Kelley, "In Praise of Followers," 147.

11. Kelley posits a fifth type of follower, *Survivors*. Such people have learned to respond in ways that meet the approval of those in charge; they are well-suited for weathering changes in leadership. However, to the degree to which they are simply following the implicit or explicit directives of the leader, they are best described as "sheep" who are critical thinkers (or not) and active (or passive) because that is what is expected. See "In Praise of Followers," 145.

12. Patsy Baker Blackshear, "The Followership Continuum: A Model for Increasing Organizational Productivity," *The Innovation Journal: The Public Sector Innovation Journal* 9, no. 1 (2004): article 7, http://www.innovation.cc/discussion-papers/9_1_7_blackshear_innovation_works-emp.pdf.

13. Ibid., 6.

14. Ibid., 6–7.

15. Ibid., 13–14.

16. Ibid., 13.

17. One of the earliest schema, proposed by Abraham Zaleznik and published in 1965, describes subordinates in terms of whether they were active or passive and dominant or submissive; he describes four types: impulsive, compulsive, masochistic, and withdrawn. Clearly, not a very positive read of followers, Zaleznik seemed to be emphasizing the dysfunctional rather than the functional. See "The Dynamics of Subordinacy," *Harvard Business Review* (May/June 1965):119–32. Another more recent typology is set up by Ira Chaleff in *The Courageous Follower* (San Francisco: Barrett-Koeher, 2005) in which he proposes a grid based on levels of support the follower gives the leader and levels to which the follower is willing to challenge the leader. His four types are Implementer, Partner, Individualist, and Resource. A third schema proposed by Barbara Kellerman "divides all followers into five different types, according to where they fall along a continuum that ranges from feeling and doing absolutely nothing on the one end to being passionately committed and deeply involved on the other. The five types are Isolate, Bystander, Participant, Activist, and Diehard." *Followership: How Followers Are Creating Change and Changing Leaders* (Boston: Harvard Business Press, 2008), 83.

18. The most helpful way to develop these ideas is to look at the work of constructive developmentalists and their description of mature adulthood. For example, Robert Kegan and James Fowler, the former who examines the development of human maturity and the latter who examines the same within the context of faith development. For both authors, defining characteristics of mature adulthood rest on the capacity to step back from the received perception of the world, that is, the world into which we have been socialized. And from that perspective take on and engage in a new way with received teaching and authority that is external to ourselves. See Robert Kegan, *In Over Our Heads: The Mental Demands of Modern Life* (Boston: Harvard University Press, 1994); and James Fowler, *Stages of Faith: The Psychology of Human Development and the Quest for Meaning* (New York: Harper Collins, 1981); and *Faithful Change: The Personal and Public Challenges of Postmodern Life* (Nashville: Abingdon Press, 1996).

19. For further discussion of this expanded notion of faithfulness, see Jane Regan, "Fostering the Next Generation of Faithful Women," in

Prophetic Witness: Catholic Women's Strategies for Reform, ed. Colleen Griffith (New York: Crossroads, 2009), 140–49.

20. Particularly influential in composing this list is the writing of Ira Chaleff in *The Faithful Follower*. In many ways, his notion of the courageous follower has close resonance with the faithful follower being described here.

21. Blackshear, "The Followership Continuum," 14.

22. For example, in the case of Mass attendance, a Pew research report from 2013 stated, "The share of all Catholics who say they attend Mass at least once a week has dropped from 47% in 1974 to 24% in 2012; among [self-identified] "strong" Catholics, it has fallen more than 30 points, from 85% in 1974 to 53% last year." See http://www. pewforum.org/2013/03/13/strong-catholic-identity-at-a-four-decade-low-in-us/.

23. It is beyond what we can do here to examine the less direct impact on parish life of the cultural context within which it is situated. For example, the rise of "nones," those who claim no religious affiliation, is both a sign and a contributing factor to the cultural milieu. See Pew Research report, "Nones on the Rise," http://www.pewforum. org/2012/10/09/nones-on-the-rise/.

24. For a helpful text for examining the dynamics of change and how to support its implementation at the organizational level, see Robert Kegan and Lisa Laskow Lahey, *Immunity to Change: How to Overcome It and Unlock the Potential in Yourself and Your Organization* (Boston: Harvard Business Review, 2009).

25. This is discussed at length in chapter 5.

26. David Tracy, *Plurality and Ambiguity: Hermeneutics, Religion, Hope* (San Francisco: Harper and Row, 1987), 19.

27. While here we are talking about the follower's attitude toward the leader, it could be argued that the positive hermeneutic needs to be applied to all members of a community of practice. Without it, the kind of conversation set out in chapter 5 and the process of discernment discussed in chapter 7 are virtually impossible.

28. Chaleff, *The Faithful Follower*, 157.

29. USCCB, *Called and Gifted: The American Catholic Laity* (Washington, DC: USCCB Publishing, 1980), http://www.usccb.org/ about/laity-marriage-family-life-and-youth/laity/upload/called_and_ gifted.pdf.

CHAPTER 7

1. David Lonsdale, *Listening to the Music of the Spirit: The Art of Discernment* (Notre Dame, IN: Ave Maria Press, 1992), 49.

2. For a discussion of the role of human engagement through prayer, trust, and openness in Acts 10, see Luke Timothy Johnson, *Scripture and Discernment: Decision Making in the Church* (Nashville: Abingdon Press, 1983), 91–5.

3. Johnson, *Scripture and Discernment*, 93.

4. The debate concerning the historicity of the account in Acts is interesting but not necessarily determinant for the discussion here. See the discussion in chapter 5 of *Scripture and Discernment* in which Johnson argues that regardless of the historical accuracy of the account—what specific events precipitated the meeting, was there one meeting or two, was the decree written then or at another time—this does not take away from the possibility of reading the text today for insight into the author of Luke/Acts's understanding of the process of discernment.

5 Alex T. M. Cheung, in his essay "A Narrative Analysis of Acts 14:27–5:35: Literary Shaping in Luke's Account of the Jerusalem Council," *Westminster Theological Journal* 55 (1993): 137–54, presents an argument for the narrative consisting of four "mission reports" followed by either a dispute between Paul and those supporting Jewish law or a resolution. The story concludes with the final resolution (15:13ff.) where James addresses the gathering.

6. James cites Amos 9:11–12.

7. Avery Dulles, "An Ecclesial Model for Theological Reflection: The Council of Jerusalem," in *Tracing the Spirit: Communities, Social Action, and Theological Reflection*, ed. James Hug (New York: Paulist Press, 1983), 225.

8. Johnson, *Scripture and Discernment*, 104.

9. Wilkie Au and Noreen Cannon Au, *The Discerning Heart* (New York: Paulist Press, 2006), 19.

10. Ibid., 50.

11. Within the context of Ignatian spirituality, this is the process by which we are aware of consolation and desolation. A helpful resource on consolation and desolation and their role in discernment can be found in

Mark Thibodeaux, *God's Voice Within: The Ignatian Way to Discover God's Will* (Chicago: Loyola Press, 2010).

12. Annie Dillard, *The Writing Life* (San Francisco: Harper and Row, 1989), 32.

13. Elizabeth Liebert, *The Way of Discernment: Spiritual Practices for Decision Making* (Louisville: Westminster/John Knox, 2008), 23.

14. Here, I am drawing on the notion of "limit situations," those times when we are aware of either the limits of our lives (i.e., those times in which we are aware of our limitations as created beings expressed most distinctly in sin and mortality) and the limits for our lives (i.e., those times in which we are aware of the expansiveness of our lives within the created order and ultimately in God). See David Tracy, *Blessed Rage for Order* (New York: The Seabury Press, 1975). He writes,

> Fundamentally, the concept refers to those human situations wherein a human being ineluctably finds manifest a certain ultimate limit or horizon to his or her existence. The concept itself is mediated by "showing" the implications of certain crucial positive and negative experiential limit-situations. More exactly, limit-situations refer to two basic kinds of existential situation: either those "boundary" situations of guilt, anxiety, sickness, and the recognition of death as one's own destiny, or those situations called "ecstatic experiences"—intense joy, love, reassurance, creation. All genuine limit-situations refer to those experiences, both positive and negative, wherein we both experience our own human limits (limit-to) as our own as well as recognize, however haltingly, some disclosure of a limit-of our experience. (105)

15. Referred to as "Awareness Examen," one of the clearest and simplest expressions of this is in Liebert, *The Way of Discernment*, 3–4.

16. I am drawing primarily on Liebert, *The Way of Discernment*; see pages 19–21 for the steps she proposes. They are then examined in the remaining chapters of her book.

17. Thibodeaux, *God's Voice Within*, 196–97.

18. Frank Rogers, "Discernment," in *Practicing Our Faith: A Way of Life for a Searching People*, ed. Dorothy C. Bass (San Francisco: Jossey-Bass, 1997), 113.

19. For further discussion of characteristics or dynamics essential to effective communal discernment, see Lonsdale, *Listening to the Music of the Spirit*, 135. Also, Nancy E. Bedford, "Little Moves against Destructiveness: Theology and the Practice of Discernment," in *Practicing Theology: Beliefs and Practices in Christian Life*, ed. Miroslav Volf and Dorothy C. Bass (Grand Rapids, MI: Eerdmans, 2002), 170–71.

20. See chapter 3, pages 61–63.

BIBLIOGRAPHY

ECCLESIAL DOCUMENTS

Congregation for the Clergy. *General Directory for Catechesis* (1998). http://www.vatican.va/roman_curia/congregations/cclergy/documents/rc_con_ccatheduc_doc_17041998_directory-for-catechesis_en.html.

Documents of Vatican Council II. *Ad Gentes* (AG), "On the Missionary Activity of the Church" (1965). http://www.vatican.va/archive/hist_councils/ii_vatican_council/documents/vat-ii_decree_19651207_ad-gentes_en.html.

Documents of Vatican Council II. *Lumen Gentium* (LG), "The Dogmatic Constitution on the Church" (1964). http://www.vatican.va/archive/hist_councils/ii_vatican_council/documents/vat-ii_const_19641121_lumen-gentium_en.html.

Pope Francis. *Evangelii Gaudium* (EG), "The Joy of the Gospel" (2013). http://www.vatican.va/holy_father/francesco/apost_exhortations/documents/papa-francesco_esortazione-ap_20131124_evangelii-gaudium_en.html.

Pope John Paul II. *Catechesi Tradendae* (CT), "Apostolic Exhortation on Catechesis" (1979). http://www.vatican.va/holy_father/john_paul_ii/apost_exhortations/documents/hf_jp-ii_exh_16101979_catechesi-tradendae_en.html.

———. *Christifideles Laici* (CL), "Apostolic Exhortation on the Laity" (1988). http://www.vatican.va/holy_father/john_paul_ii/apost_exhortations/documents/hf_jp-ii_exh_30121988_christifideles-laici_en.html.

———. *Redemptoris Missio* (RM), "On the Church's Mission Activity" (1990). http://www.vatican.va/holy_father/john_paul_ii/encyclicals/documents/hf_jp-ii_enc_07121990_redemptoris-missio_en.html.

Pope Paul VI. *Evangelii Nuntiandi* (EN), "Apostolic Exhortation on Evangelization" (1975). http://www.vatican.va/holy_fath er/paul_vi/apost_exhortations/documents/hf_p-vi_exh_19751208_evangelii-nuntiandi_en.html.

USCCB. *Called and Gifted: The American Catholic Laity.* Washington, DC: USCCB Publishing, 1980. http://www.usccb.org/about/laity-marriage-family-life-and-youth/laity/upload/called_and_gifted.pdf.

———. *Called and Gifted for the Third Millennium.* Washington, DC: USCCB Publishing, 1995.

———. *Our Hearts Were Burning Within Us.* Washington, DC: USCCB Publishing, 1999.

GENERAL BIBLIOGRAPHY

Arterbury, Andrew E. *Entertaining Angels: Early Christian Hospitality in its Mediterranean Setting.* Sheffield: Sheffield Phoenix, 2005.

Au, Wilkie, and Noreen Cannon Au. *The Discerning Heart.* Mahwah, NJ: Paulist Press, 2006.

Baker, Susan D. "Followership: The Theoretical Foundation of a Contemporary Construct." *Journal of Leadership and Organizational Studies* 14, no.1 (2007): 50–60.

Bass, Dorothy C. *Practicing Our Faith: A Way of Life for a Searching People.* The Practices of Faith Series. San Francisco: Jossey-Bass, 2009.

Bedford, Nancy E. "Little Moves against Destructiveness: Theology and the Practice of Discernment." In *Practicing Theology: Beliefs and Practices in Christian Life*, edited by Miroslav Volf and Dorothy C. Bass, 157–83. Grand Rapids, MI: Eerdmans, 2002.

Bibliography

Bjugstad, Kent, et al. "A Fresh Look at Followership: A Model for Matching Followership and Leadership Styles." *Journal of Behavioral and Applied Management* 7 (April 2006): 304–19.

Blackshear, Patsy Baker. "The Followership Continuum: A Model for Increasing Organizational Productivity." *The Innovation Journal: The Public Sector Innovation Journal* 9, no. 1 (2004): article 7. http://www.innovation.cc/discussion-papers/9_1_7_blackshear_innovation_works-emp.pdf.

Brackley, Dean. *The Call to Discernment in Troubled Times: New Perspectives on the Transformative Wisdom of Ignatius of Loyola.* New York: The Crossroad Publishing Company, 2004.

Bretherton, Luke. *Hospitality as Holiness: Christian Witness amid Moral Diversity.* Burlington, VT: Ashgate, 2006.

Brown, John Seely, Allan Collins, and Paul Duguid. "Situated Cognition and the Culture of Learning." In *Situated Learning Perspectives*, edited by Hilary McLellan, 19–44. Englewood Cliffs, NJ: Educational Technology Publications, 1996.

Brown, John Seely, and Paul Duguid. "Organizational Learning and Communities-of-Practice: Toward a Unified View of Working, Learning, and Innovation." *Organization Science* 2, no. 1 (1991): 40–57.

———. "Stolen Knowledge." In *Situated Learning Perspectives*, edited by Hilary McLellan, 47–56. Englewood Cliffs, NJ: Educational Technology Publications, 1996.

Brown, Raymond. *The Gospel according to John I-XII.* Anchor Bible Series 29. Garden City, NY: Doubleday, 1966.

Burbles, Nicholas, and Suzanne Rice. "Dialogue across Differences: Continuing the Conversation." *Harvard Business Review* 61, no. 4 (1991): 393–416.

Carsten, Melissa K., et al., "Exploring Social Construction of Followership: A Qualitative Study." *The Leadership Quarterly* 21 (2010): 543–62.

Chaleff, Ira. *The Courageous Follower.* San Francisco: Barrett-Koeher, 2005.

Cheung, Alex T. M. "A Narrative Analysis of Acts 14:27–15:35: Literary Shaping in Luke's Account of the Jerusalem Council." *Westminster Theological Journal* 55 (1993): 137–54.

Cobb, Paul, and Janet Bowers. "Cognitive and Situated Learning Perspectives in Theory and Practice." *Educational Researchers* 28 (1999): 4–15.

Collinson, David. "Rethinking Followership: A Post-structuralist Analysis of Follower Identities." *The Leadership Quarterly* 17 (2006): 179–89.

Contu, A., and H. Willmott. "Re-embedding Situatedness: The Importance of Power Relations in Learning Theory." *Organization Science* 14, no. 3 (2003): 283–96.

DeMay, P., and J. Haers, eds. *Theology and Conversation: Towards a Relational Theology*. Leuven: Leuven University Press, 2003.

Dillard, Annie. *The Writing Life*. San Francisco: Harper and Row, 1989.

Dulles, Avery. "An Ecclesial Model for Theological Reflection: The Council of Jerusalem." In *Tracing the Spirit: Communities, Social Action, and Theological Reflection*, edited by James Hug, 218–41. New York: Paulist Press, 1983.

———. "John Paul II and the New Evangelization." *America* 166, no. 3 (1992): 52–59, 69–72.

Dykstra, Craig. "A Theological Understanding of Christian Practices." *Lifelong Faith* (Summer 2008).

Fowler, James. *Faithful Change: The Personal and Public Challenges of Postmodern Life*. Nashville: Abingdon Press, 1996.

———. *Stages of Faith: The Psychology of Human Development and the Quest for Meaning*. New York: Harper Collins, 1981.

Freire, Paulo. *Pedagogy of the Oppressed*. New York and London: Bloomsbury Academic, 2012.

Gadamer, Hans Georg. *Truth and Method*. 2nd ed. New York: Continuum, 1999.

Gaillardetz, Richard R. *The Church in the Making:* Lumen gentium, Christus dominus, Orientalium ecclesiarum. Mahwah, NJ: Paulist Press, 2006.

———. *Ecclesiology for a Global Church: A People Called and Sent.* Theology in Global Perspectives. Maryknoll, NY: Orbis Books, 2008.

Gittins, Anthony J. *A Presence that Disturbs: A Call to Radical Discipleship.* St. Louis, MO: Liguori, 2002.

Gleeson, Brian. "Commemorating *Lumen Gentium*: A Short History of a Ground-breaking Charter." *Australian eJournal of Theology* (August 3, 2004). http://aejt.com.au/__data/assets/pdf_file/0006/395655/AEJT_3.12_Gleeson.pdf.

Griffith, Collen, ed. *Prophetic Witness: Catholic Women's Strategies for Reform.* New York: Crossroad Publishing, 2009.

Groome, Thomas. *Sharing Faith.* San Francisco: Harper, 1991.

———. *Will There Be Faith? – A New Vision for Educating and Growing Disciples.* San Francisco: HarperOne, 2011.

Groome, Thomas, and Harold Horell, eds. *Horizons and Hopes: The Future of Religious Education.* Mahwah, NJ: Paulist Press, 2003.

Gula, Richard M. *Moral Discernment.* Mahwah, NJ: Paulist Press, 1997.

Hansman, Catherine A. "Adult Learning in Communities of Practice: Situating Theory in Practice." In *Communities of Practice: Creating Learning Environments for Educators,* edited by Paul Hildreth, Chris Kimble, Isabell Bourdon, 293–309. Charlotte: Information Age Publishing, 2008.

Harrington, Daniel. *Meeting St. John Today: Understanding the Man, His Mission, and His Message.* Chicago: Loyola, 2011.

Harrington, Daniel, and Thomas Stegman, "John's Gospel: Holy Week and Easter Themes," Encore video, posted by School of Theology and Ministry, Boston College, March 23, 2012, http://www.bc.edu/schools/stm/edevnts/CampusEvents/PastLectures/2012/3-23-12_4.html.

Hay, Kenneth E. "Legitimate Peripheral Participation, Instructionism and Constructionism: Whose Situation Is It Anyway?" In *Situated Learning Perspectives*, edited by Hilary McLellan, 89–98. Englewood Cliffs, NJ: Educational Technology Publications, 1996.

Hinze, Bradford E. *Practices of Dialogue in the Roman Catholic Church: Aims and Obstacles, Lessons and Laments*. New York: Continuum, 2006.

Hughes, Jason, et al., eds. *Communities of Practice: Critical Perspective*. New York: Routledge, 2007.

Isaacs, William. *Dialogue and the Art of Thinking Together*. New York: Currency, 1999.

Johnson, Luke Timothy. *Scripture and Discernment: Decision Making in the Church*. Nashville: Abingdon Press, 1983.

Jones, L. Gregory. "Eucharistic Hospitality: Welcoming the Stranger into the Household of God." *The Reformed Journal* 39, no. 3 (1989): 12–17.

Kegan, Robert. *In over Our Heads: The Mental Demands of Modern Life*. Boston: Harvard University Press, 1994.

Kegan, Robert, and Lisa Laskow Lahey. *How the Way We Talk Can Change the Way We Work: Seven Languages for Transformation*. San Francisco: Jossey-Bass, 2001.

Kellerman, Barbara. *Followership: How Followers Are Creating Change and Changing Leaders*. Boston: Harvard Business Press, 2008.

Kelley, Robert E. "In Praise of Followers." *Harvard Business Review* 66 (1988): 142–48.

Kimble, Chris, and Paul Hildreth, eds. *Communities of Practice: Creating Learning Environments for Educators*. Charlotte, NC: Information Age, 2008.

Koenig, John. *New Testament Hospitality: Partnership with Strangers as Promise and Mission*. Philadelphia: Fortress Press, 1985.

Kropf, Marlene. "Cultivating a Congregational Climate of Discernment." *Vision* (2011): 43–51.

Bibliography

Lakeland, Paul. *The Liberation of the Laity*. New York: Bloomsbury Academic, 2004.

Latour, Sharon, and Vicki Rast. "Dynamic Followership: The Prerequisite for Effective Leadership." *Air and Space Power Journal* (Winter 2004): 102–10.

Lave, Jean, and Etienne Wenger. *Situated Learning: Legitimate Peripheral Participation*. New York: Cambridge University Press, 1991.

Liebert, Elizabeth. *The Way of Discernment: Spiritual Practices for Decision Making*. Louisville, KY: Westminster/John Knox, 2008.

Lonsdale, David. *Listening to the Music of the Spirit: The Art of Discernment*. Notre Dame, IN: Ave Maria Press, 1992.

MacIntyre, Alasdair. *After Virtue*. 3rd ed. Notre Dame: University of Notre Dame Press, 2007.

Mathews, Kenneth A. *The New American Commentary*, vol. 1b. Nashville: Broadman and Holmen, 2005.

McGregor, Peter John. "New World, New Pentecost, New Church." *Compass* 12, no. 5 (2012): 18–31.

McLellan, Hilary, ed. *Situated Learning Perspectives*. Englewood Cliffs, NJ: Educational Technology Publications, 1996.

Moloney, Francis J., and Daniel J. Harrington. *Gospel of John*. Sacra Pagina series 4. Collegeville, MN: Liturgical Press, 1998.

Morgan, Hampton. "Remember to Show Hospitality: A Sign of Grace in Graceless Times." *International Review of Mission* 87, no. 347 (1998): 535–39.

Mutch, Alistair. "Communities of Practice and Habitus: A Critique." *Organization Studies* 24, no. 3 (2003): 383–401.

O'Neil, John. "On Schools as Learning Organizations: A Conversation with Peter Senge." *Self-renewing Schools* 52, no. 7 (April 1995): 20–23. http://patriciathinks.yolasite.com/resources/Senge.pdf.

Palmer, Parker J. *The Company of Strangers: Christians and the Renewal of America's Public Life*. New York: Crossroad Publishing, 1983.

Pohl, Christine D. *Making Room: Recovering Hospitality as a Christian Tradition.* Grand Rapids, MI: Wm. B. Eerdmans, 1999.

Rakoczy, Susan W. "Transforming the Tradition of Discernment." *Journal of Theology for Southern Africa* 139 (March 2011): 91–109.

Regan, Jane E. *Forming a Community of Faith: A Guide to Success in Adult Faith Formation Today.* Mystic, CT: Twenty Third Publications, 2014.

———. *Toward an Adult Church: A Vision of Faith Formation.* Chicago: Loyola Press, 2002.

Regan, Jane E., and Michael P. Horan. *Good News in New Forms.* Washington, DC: National Conference of Catechetical Leaders, 2000.

Richard, Lucien. *Living the Hospitality of God.* Mahwah, NJ: Paulist Press, 2000.

Rogers, Frank. "Discernment." In *Practicing Our Faith: A Way of Life for a Searching People*, edited by Dorothy C. Bass, 105–18. San Francisco: Jossey-Bass, 1997.

Russell, Letty M. *Just Hospitality: God's Welcome in a World of Difference.* Edited by J. Shannon Clarkson and Kate M. Ott. Louisville, KY: WJK Press, 2009.

Rymarz, Richard. "John Paul II and the 'New Evangelization': Origins and Meaning." *Australian eJournal of Theology* 15 (2010), http://aejt.com.au/__data/assets/pdf_file/0009/225396/Rymarcz_evangelization_GH.pdf.

———. "The New Evangelization in an Ecclesiological Context." *The Heythrop Journal* 52 (2011): 772–84.

Saint-Onge, Hubert, and Debra Wallace. *Leveraging Communities of Practice for Strategic Advantage.* Boston: Butterworth-Heinemann, 2003.

Schwöbel, Christoph. "God as Conversation: Reflection on a Theological Ontology of Communicative Relations." In *Theology and Conversation: Towards a Relational Theology*, edited by P. DeMay and J. Haers, 43–68. Leuven: Leuven University Press, 2003.

Senge, Peter. *The Fifth Discipline: The Art and Practice of Learning Organizations*. New York: Currency/Doubleday, 1990.

Tanner, Deborah. *The Argument Culture: Moving from Debate to Dialogue*. New York: Random House, 1998.

Tomkinson, Raymond. *Called to Love: Discernment, Decision Making and Ministry*. London: SCM Press, 2012.

Tracy, David. *The Analogical Imagination: Christian Theology and the Culture of Pluralism*. New York: Crossroad Publishing, 1998.

———. *Plurality and Ambiguity: Hermeneutics, Religion, Hope*. San Francisco: Harper and Row, 1987.

Tusting, Karin. "Language and Power in Communities of Practice." In *Beyond Communities of Practice: Language, Power and Social Context*, edited by Barton and Tusting, 36–54. New York: Cambridge University Press, 2005.

Wenger, Etienne. "Communities of Practice and Social Learning Systems." *Organization* 7, no. 2 (2000): 225–46.

———. "Communities of Practice and Social Learning Systems: The Career of a Concept." In *Social Learning Systems and Communities of Practice*, edited by Chris Blackmore, 179–98. London: Springer, 2010.

———. *Communities of Practice: Learning, Meaning and Identity*. Cambridge University Press, 1998.

Wenger, Etienne, Richard A. McDermott, and William Snyder. *Cultivating Communities of Practice: a Guide to Managing Knowledge*. Boston, MA: Harvard Business School Press, 2002.

Zaleznik, Abraham. "The Dynamics of Subordinacy." *Harvard Business Review* 41 (1965): 119–32.